New Cross-Fucked Musings on a Manic Reality: Nonfiction of the Enigmatic Polygeneration

Edited by
Tom Bradley

New Cross-Fucked Musings on a Manic Reality:
Nonfiction of the Enigmatic Polygeneration
Editor: Tom Bradley, tombradley.org

Cover art:
"Personal Demon"

Editor portrait:

First edition published by

Dog Horn Publishing
6 Athlone Terrace
Armley
Leeds
LS12 1UA

editor@doghornpublishing.com
doghornpublishing.com

ISBN: 978-1-907133-15-2

All effort has been made to seek permissions for quotes and provide adequate referencing for essays. If you feel proper attribution has not been given, please contact us and we will rectify the issue.

Table of Contents

Editor's Introduction

Who are the Enigmatic Polygeneration?

from *Put It Down in a Book* (The Drill Press, 2009)

In a creation where particles can spookily act upon each other at a distance of quadrillions of light years, the seven ages of man are as days in the week, and a generation can span an open-ended number of decades.

When a school of scribblers eschews congregation at a specific longitude-latitude, what the PR folks call "the presentation self" gets wholesomely idealized. To the same degree that carefully drafted prose sails above extempore gab, the quality of schmoozing becomes enhanced. When, to paraphrase Hugh Fox, the *Who gets unsecured by landscape*, all the somatic curses of generated existence are stripped away. Once space has been erased by the miracle of email, so has time, in terms of its effects on the human frame.

The envy inspired by exquisitely smooth foreheads and cheeks; the superciliousness engendered by wrinkles and arthritic gaits; the mutual revulsion that results in commingling the disparate B.O.s of maturity and im-; the disharmony of voices cracked with senectitude and late teen hormones; the ambiguous eros ignited when the androgyne grace of late adolescence rubs against grizzled moobs; the subcortical whiffs of the Freudian family-disease that obtrude on every animal awareness when figures substitutable for parent and spawn rub elbows, when personal encounters take place among people separable by more than a sibling's number of years — none of this signifies through the hermetic medium of the internet.

In a universe ruled by karma and rebirth, "generation" is a bad word, denoting as it does the stifling of spirits in coats of crass skin, the greatest disservice that can be done. Nevertheless, Hugh Fox got to christen the Invisible Generation, Andrew Gallix the Offbeats. So I'll invent a name to embrace these people. I'll make it doubly apt, as they produce electricity as well as useful heat:

the enigmatic polygeneration.

John-Ivan Palmer

Sodom in Half:
Ricki Hilliard, Lost King of the Blue Ventriloquists

I went from psych major at UC Berkeley to Felicia Fantasy's Tenderloin boyfriend in one academic quarter. If I hadn't traded the soporific lecture hall for the strip club dressing room, I might never have heard of Ricki Hilliard, the most notorious of the blue room vents.

Successful ventriloquists working today, like Todd Oliver (with his live talking dog), or Bob Trent (with his smart-ass crow), can only remember a few blue vents by name. There was Wayne Roland in Chicago, who tried to break out of blue rooms, but still did risque material and was always in trouble for it. There was Grover Ruwe, the sly jape from Kansas City, Dick Weston in Vegas, and Richard and Willey (who Trent calls "wickedly dirty"). Barklay Shaw's X-rated chicken and Wayland Flowers' dirty old lady dummy all worked — again in Trent's words — "really blue." But almost nobody's heard of Ricki Hilliard. He was too blue.

When we delve into the world of XXX-rated ventriloquism, we delve into such a black hole of human taboo that nothing radiates out. Oblivion gobbles up the names.

There is no mention of blue room vents in Valentine Vox's definitive *I Can See Your Lips Moving, The History and Art of Ventriloquism* (1981). I talk to agents like Gilbert Miller in Las Vegas, who knows everything about show biz from vaudeville to the point where it all turned to shit. He can't remember the name of a single dirty vent. Not only that, but he bristles at the very mention of filthy ventriloquists and distances himself in such a way that I feel ashamed I ever asked. The taboo is as strong now as in the 13th century when ventriloquists were tortured and executed by Christian authorities for the capital crime of making a voice appear to originate from someplace other than its source.

And I use the terms "dirty" and "filthy" not to be judgmental, but because these were the terms used both inside and outside the business itself. It assumes the modal values of the culture as a constant, and the modifiers and enhancers measure just how far from mainstream taste you can expect the dummy to stray. *You want a dirty disgusting vent act, utterly, and I mean UTTERLY filthy?* That sort of thing. It's a way to get directly to the point and do a little business.

What made Ricki Hilliard such a morsel of the forgotten wasn't just the standard blue vent gimmicks, the filthy jokes, the dummy's erection, the urination into the audience, the raised finger, the endless fuck, fuck, fuck. That alone would have guaranteed him work inversely proportional to his importance in ventriloquial history. It wasn't because he merged two historical no-no's: cultural taboo and making inanimate objects appear conscious (although that may be closer to the necromantic essence of his demonic power). He was devastatingly popular in west coast strip clubs of the lowest order for five short years because he dredged deeper, took greater risks, and consorted with more ancient gods than any known ventriloquist for the last three thousand years.

Hilliard began his career in Tenderloin porn theaters, doing ten minute shows between movies to give the projectionist time to switch reels. It was an impossible niche, and why he did it rather than work, let's say, kiddie shows, is part of Hilliard's mystery. When the lights went up, Hilliard walked out on the stage carrying the dummy with a penis sticking out. It was an atrocious sight gag, but it worked. Hilliard himself looked straight and wholesome, a kind of skinny dork. The dummy was a bug-eyed Charlie Manson figure, nearly full human size, which made the erection gimmick all the more "realistic."

Most blue room vents were products of the 1950's, when booming Rust Belt factories all had Men's Clubs that threw parties with strippers and dirty comics. This was long before the Devil went PC. Several times a year Puritanism gave way to Paganism and life seemed more balanced and eternal than it does today. Hundreds of acts and agents thrived in this culture like bread mold and blue vents worked circuits year round. But by the early 1970's most were ravaged by vice and life on the road.

With my library and files on cognitive psychology and everything I never learned in class, I moved to Turk St. with Felicia Fantasy and her snake. I don't know if anyone's written the intellectual history of the Tenderloin, but there was one. The cheap hotels along Eddy, O'Farrell and Turk Streets were indeed filled with garden variety losers. But peppered among them were people like me, the rejects of formal education, who wouldn't follow the syllabus-bizarre bookworms, amphetamine-addicted students of metaphysical poetry, erotomaniacal biblical scholars, socially crippled botanists, perversion seeking poets. Ricki Hilliard was among them, run out of Chicago, according to rumor, by some scandal in the Shakespearean theater clique. All these seekers of odd flavors and fragrances were too nonconformist for the middle class hippies, so they ended up in the Tenderloin, which was no love-in. As my behaviorist professors would put it, positive and negative reinforcement in a maximum displacement from zero. Violence was always imminent. You saw it in the doors, most of which had been repaired numerous times from being kicked in by police or people going berserk. Tenderloin doors were always old, the locks were always new. You had to fight for your ecstasy. Kicking was the name of the game. Get yer kicks, kick the junk, kick yer ass, what a kick. People just stepped over the blood on the sidewalk. It had to be as disturbing to Hilliard as it was to me. All night the screams and the sirens made it difficult to sleep, and when you did sleep you had nightmares. X-rated ventriloquism was how Hilliard kicked his way out of hell.

I saw Hilliard in Tenderloin pross bars doing funny voices for hookers, or on the North Beach strip where he knew all the sex shop clerks. He tried to get himself booked at Big Al's, the Condor, etc. He did work some of the lesser clubs on a one shot basis, but no one wanted to pay him. I even saw him on Market Street a few times, once in the rain, pathetically working for tips. Whenever I complimented him on his thespian talents, he used his hip, loose, show biz persona to take control of the conversation to pry sexual information out of me. Would I screw a cow for a thousand dollars? A million? He'd manipulate me into some absurd hypothetical agreement, then spend days telling everyone about it, building the whole thing into an offstage routine, voices and all. And here's what the cow said . . . etc. No one could get close to him because he used ventriloquism as a shield. When things got personal, he'd throw a voice into a shot glass or a hash pipe or a hooker's cleavage. He was definitely in a self-referential world of his own and unless it involved some kind of sexual commerce most people avoided him.

When my girlfriend, the ultra-high maintenance, all-nude sensation, Felicia Fantasy, finally got him on the peeler circuit, we bumped into him all the time in places like the Palm Tree Lounge in Calgary, The Syndicate and Fantasia Cabaret in Edmonton, The King of Hearts in Laramie, and the Roxy in Cheyenne before they shut it down as a public nuisance.

In show biz, especially tough show biz, evolution happens quickly. Laughs aren't that easy to get. In roadhouse hells of vomit, drool, blood and ugly scenes, you'll do anything for laughs. You'll steal jokes, you'll score them like guns and drugs, you'll run your mind at full throttle and drive everyone nuts in a mad quest for workable lines. If you fail, you die. That's why show business thrives on the metaphors of violence. You kill em, you slay em, you knock em dead. Or you die. Hilliard mowed em down-about half the time.

The sight gags were pretty much the high point of the show. One of the dummy's hands had the middle finger permanently out and the arm worked on a rod controlled by Hilliard so the dummy was constantly flipping people off. Fuck you, fuck you, fuck you, and by the way, fuck you too. It was a formula of cosmic simplicity. In the Rocky Mountain cowboy dumps in the winter of 1970, I saw Hilliard's act literally explode with adaptive mechanisms. In addition to the erection gimmick, he rigged up a big glob of brown clay to drop out the dummy's ass. Hilliard's logic, if not his taste, was flawless — a defecating ventriloquist dummy. Then sometime between the Dragon Lounge in Portland and the Frontier Room in Vancouver, Hilliard figured out a way to pack pounds and pounds of clay into the oversized dummy's body, so much that the issue came down to how much *weight* Hilliard could carry out onto the stage. The more the shats, the more the laughs. He dropped the stuff in laps, on people's heads. He was a bouncer's nightmare. Felicia complained about clay causing embarrassing stains on her costumes when she rolled around on the floor and put a lot of pressure on *me* to get Hilliard to stop. There were other hostilities. Drunks threw clay back at the dummy (but never Hilliard). Several times he had to be escorted to his car because someone threatened to kick the dummy's ass (never Hilliard's) in the parking lot. In a medium of Dionysian excess it flipped a switch in the collective unconscious, and on these nights I could see why, for 30 centuries, ventriloquism could be such a dangerous activity.

In some ways it was amazing to see. The shock, the hysterics, the revulsion. After about 10 minutes of overkill from his crapping dummy, he brought out the big finish — a potty-mouthed female dummy rigged up with a dress that came off. He probably stole the idea from blue room vent Chris Cross. But Hilliard took it one step further. Not only did the female dummy have pubic hair, but a kind of opening so you could actually peer inside her artificial body. The dummy wench conned some stooge up on stage to look between her legs, which were rigged up to open real wide or snap shut. Catcallers yelled, "Whata ya see!" No matter what the guy said, it was funny. Meanwhile, during all of this, the dummy insulted the stooge. Pure genius.

If the trends would have stayed the same, Hilliard might still be doing it. He might even have become another Lenny Bruce or Andy Kaufman. But west coast strip clubs in the early 1970's were vaudeville's absolute and final dead end. Generic crab walkers and butt puppets, who'd show more and work for less, ran strippers out of business almost overnight, including my girlfriend, the Snake Dancing Wonder. I have no idea where all these people went. They seemed to vanish in some great mass extinction. I never saw Felicia again after that incident in Omaha, when she kicked me out of her car and drove off to Denver with a bunch of my books on the nature of consciousness. I never saw them again either.

Clubs went through a quick succession of fads from male strippers to stage hypnotism, disco, mud wrestling and then comedy clubs created a whole new format. Vaudeville literally went out in a blaze of glory. Suspicious fires were commonplace.

The last time I saw Ricki Hilliard was in the sleaziest toilet of all time, the Kon Tiki Lounge on highway 290 between Spokane and Coeur d'Alene. It was an awful week. Felicia said the only reason she brought me on the road with her was because she needed a driver, otherwise she hated me and by the way, would I drive her to Omaha? Hilliard was stabbed by an Indian he outraged with his shitting dummy and spent the night in a hospital. I found out he had an eight year old son in Chicago no one would let him see. One night in the house trailer behind the club, I heard him through the thin walls crying hysterically. Since then someone told me he was in porno movies, someone else said he was arrested in a john sweep in Seattle, and another rumor had him breaking a two week contract in Anchorage because of some scandal that forced him to leave town suddenly. But all of it was hearsay. Trying to verify the facts surrounding traveling night club acts is like trying to find the real Jesus.

Wayne Roland died an alcoholic born-again Christian, Grover Ruwe is a born-again Christian of advanced age working for free in nursing homes, and other blue vents have died of AIDS. I have good reason to believe that Ricki Hilliard was not even his real name. Maybe somewhere in America today he's on-stage as a chillingly convincing Caliban or Richard III. Maybe he's getting stoned with Long Dong Silver.

I always thought that Hilliard was more a function of the Tenderloin than of show business. Ventriloquism for him was a survival mechanism to deter predators real or imagined, like the pika, a rabbit-like West Coast rodent that throws its voice when it hears you coming and makes rocks sound like goats. Go ahead, eat one. Meanwhile, I'm outa here.

Beyond that you could regard Ricki Hilliard as an anomalous phenomenon of no value whatsoever, like a ball of light that comes in your back door, follows you upstairs, wanders in and out of the bathroom, only to pass out a bedroom window and explode over the wisterias.

John-Ivan Palmer is a pathological liar living off the ransom he received years ago under the name of D.B. Cooper. His novel about male strippers, *Motels of Burning Madness*, was recently published by The Drill Press. For security reasons his current whereabouts is a secret.

Hugh Fox

from What Do You Do on Sundays?

My mother, in a sense, was the world's most frantic social climber. She wanted to put Cicero and her Jewish mother and whole Jewish family behind her. Escape from little bungalows in Cicero to Tudor mansions in Kenilworth and Oak Park, the fancy suburbs around.

She never made it. They felt they couldn't afford the South Shore Country Club so they joined the Swedish Club instead. Couldn't afford a house, so they lived in apartments forever and forever. Couldn't this, couldn't that . . . .and I was supposed to go to medical school, become a specialist in something, marry some fancy, rich girl, and make it <u>for them</u>.

My grandmother's whole family was totally wiped out, erased, buried, but we used to spend lots of holidays with the Irish side of the family.

Irish seemed to be OK with my mother. That's why I was sent to Leo High School in Chicago'; it was run by the Irish Christian brothers. She had nothing against her father being Irish, it was just that streetcar conductor's uniform.

My mother's father had had one brother, Frank Mangan, who lived up on the northwest side of Chicago, which was just a working class neighborhood back fifty or sixty years ago, but which more recently has gotten snobbish and yuppyish. Around Armitage.

Frank Mangan had had Rheumatic Fever when he was a kid and it had not only affected his joints (rheumatism, hence the name of the disease) but his heart . . . .and he was grey, grey, grey. Like he'd been dusted over with charcoal. He'd be always sitting there like a little old opposum in the corner of the living room when we went to visit.

He had a daughter, Lil, this huge, big-busted woman with this big round face and all kinds of frizzy hair who had a voice like a trombone (in the upper registers):

"Well, it's good to see you all. Little Hughie, howya doin'?"

And her husband, Jim, Jim Vincent, this huge-armed truck-driver for Armour and Co., the guy who carried the sides of beef into the meat markets, would always lift me up and toss me around a little, like I was some kind of little doll or something.

There was an Aunt Annie too, crippled, kind of a crippled midget, always looking up at you from the floor, hardly able to get around, but the one thing that wasn't crippled was her mouth.

"I've never seen so much snow. I was just telling Jim that we'd be better off in Alaska, on the coast. Being on the coast makes a big difference. Although I wouldn't mind Florida. Helen, you and Hugh go down to Florida a lot, don't you? How is it? All those hurricanes. Have you ever been in a hurricane? I don't know if there's ever been a hurricane in Chicago. I think the big buildings must stop hurricanes from forming. What we seem to specialize in is big snow storms. I haven't been downtown in years. Is Marshall Fields still there . . . ?"

On and on and on.

She'd been dropped on her back when she was a kid. Or fallen out of a second story window or off a back porch . . . . . .

Was she Jim Vincent's sister? I think so.

Two kids, Teresa Mary and Jimmy Vincent.

Teresa Mary always had her eye on me and I always had my eye on her. When she reached puberty she got pregnant (of course) and had a baby and started writing me little notes, and my mother got all riled up.

"Cheap little whore that she is, just let her keep away from my son. I have better things in mind for him than her!"

But there was always talk about the Kirbys, the Kirbys, the Kirbys.

"From England!" my mother would say as if that canonized them or something. Some relatives of my dead grandfather.

I mean the Vincents were pretty solidly working class. No big deal. They had nothing to do with my mother's pretentions toward royalty, her obsession with M.D.'s and big cash . . . but they were Catholic . . . .I almost said "white," as if her mother's side wasn't "white."

I guess the Irish and Anglo-Irish were OK, whatever. And it wasn't that she was anti-Jewish per se. I mean she was genuinely in love with Maurey Greiman, my father's lawyer, and when I started studying opera with Madame (always "Madame," never "Mrs.") Metzger, she invited the Metzgers over for dinner and was thrilled by them.

Fritz Metzger was funny.

He farted into an empty coke bottle and then set the gas on fire and it burned and everyone got a huge kick out of it — except my mother and Madame Metzger, who, in her own way, was just as snobbish as my mother.

I remember one time we were up on the seventh floor of the Fine Arts Building where the auditorium was, practicing for a performance of Mendelssohn's Elijah and some old janitor or something saw me and said "Hey, kid, you want to see something special?" And I said "Sure, why not?"

He took me to a door in the wall, had a key for it, opened it, and we walked across this old catwalk to another door that he opened, and in we went.

We were in some place huge, that's all I could tell, like a cathedral at night without any lights on.

"Let me see if I can find some lights."

Off he went, I heard some switches click, and BANG! On went the lights. We were in this splendid, giant auditorium, all fancy boxes and a huge stage, all Baroque, elaborate, but "in suspension," old, not falling down exactly, but just unattended, uncared for.

"This is the old auditorium. Louis Sullivan. Ever heard of him?"

"Not really."

Although years later I'd write a whole volume of poetry centered around Sullivan's architecture — Apotheosis of Olde Towne.

"This is the autorium-auditorium?" I asked, remembering piles of old opera programs my father had kept from the days when he was an usher at the "auditorium." How many times had he said "I used to bring coffee into Mary Garden's dressing room."

"This is it."

"My father used to usher here when he was in medical school."

"Beautiful place, huh?"

"Beautiful."

And we came back to the main building again and Mrs. Metzger was walking toward us down the hall holding on to the arm of this old, old lady with a cane.

Introduced the old lady with a flair of formality.

"Hugh Fox, this is my mother, Madame Mulhman, the singer. Now retired."

"My pleasure," I said and shook her trembling hand.

Years later I was reading a biography of Mahler and came across a sentence about a singer named Mulhman who had sung the soprano part in the first performance of Mahler's Das Lied Von Der Erde in Vienna at the end of the nineteenth century.

Mrs. (oops, Madame) Metzger's mother.

So Madame Metzger had her own fancy past too, didn't she?

Fancier than my Irish/Anglo-Irish ancestors.

It was a shame, when my grandmother had to leave her little bungalow in Cicero she left a whole bunch of portraits behind in the attic. No money for moving.

It was something my mother talked about endlessly later.

"All the portraits of the Kirbys. And beautiful frames too. It was a crime to leave them behind . . . . . . "

Decades later I almost went back to the old house in Cicero and asked if the present owner might just, might just have kept the portraits, or just stuck them in a corner somewhere and forgot about them. But it was so unlikely that I never pursued it.

My mother's father's brother and his family, they were kosher, but when my father did the family tree, he'd trace the Fox family back to Ireland, back to Saint Patrick, for God's sake, but my grandmother appeared without any lineage, no father or mother, no brothers or sister, just "Mary Ross [misspelled, it should have been Roos] married James Mangan."

One time when I was visiting my old pal Harry Smith in New York, I met one of his wife's cousins, this big shot Wall Street investment broker. Lunch at some club on the top of a skyscraper facing the Chrysler Building. The fanciest place I'd ever been in my life.

We started talking about being Jewish.

He was Harry's wife's cousin. The whole family was Jewish. Marion's family, the Pechiks, had had one of the *great* fortunes in pre-

World War II Czechoslovakia-Austria. They had so much money that their town-house is now the U.S. embassy in Prague.

I said something about my grandmother being Jewish.

"I can't understand it. Why the big secret? I feel cheated. Look at all the traditions, the Yiddish, the ideas, the sense of belonging to 'the tribe' that I missed out on. All my grandmother's family, the great-grandfathers and great-grandmothers and uncles and cousins I never knew. It was a kind of personal ideological holocuast. Wipe the whole thing out without a trace."

"Well, I'm not Jewish myself," he said delicately carving a little piece of ham off the big slice on his plate.

Ham was a big symbol of "liberation," wasn't it?

"What are you?"

"Episcopalian. I couldn't quite get to Catholic . . . .but almost . . . ."

"But why?"

"Because . . . ," looking around at the table next to us to be sure that no one was listening, "there was a time when *to be Jewish was to be dead*. Believe me that has a lot to do with it."

"But not in the U.S.!"

"Who knows when they came over. And in 1939 who knew who was going to win the war, the Germans seemed invincible. Besides, the whole Nazi thing went back, back, back into the late twenties . . . .."

"I remember something my Austrian-Jewish opera teacher in Chicago told us one time before class, 'You should have seen Germany at the time of the 1929 crash. You needed a wheelbarrow full of money in order to buy a loaf of bread. That's when the Nazis first surfaced.' "

"Exactly. It went back, back, back. The Jews were doing too well. And the Gernans took their sense of religious tribalism as a personal snub. And Hitler wanted the Jews' money, their property. Just look at the pictures of the Jews going to the concentration camps. Look at the faces . . . ..let's not talk about property, houses, jewelry, gold teeth . . . . . . "He stopped, tears in his eyes. "OK, OK," lifting his wine glass up, Harry and I lifting ours in response, "Lach heim, to life . . . .and let's move on to other things." A toast, nice sweet concord wine, my favorite, and, as he put his glass down, he looked out at the Chrysler Building, "Not a bad view, huh?"

"Not bad."

"Even for a Chicagoan."

"Even for a Chicagoan."

Only I don't think my mother's burying her Judaism had anything to do with Hitler and the Nazis. She felt like being Jewish was like being black. It was simply a label she didn't want anything to do with.

Like us joining the Swedish Club instead of the South Shore Country Club.

So . . . .the South Shore Country Club was more expensive. And my mother was thrilled by the fact that when I was in high school I started going out with Shirley Bourke, whose accountant father (who drove a brand new black Cadillac) belonged to the South Shore Country Club. But my parents were cheapo, cheapo, cheapo, and my father was a general practitioner in a world becoming increasingly filled with specialists, so . . . .they joined the South Side Swedish Club, and there we'd be at the smorgasboards with all the smoked fish and pickled fish and fish this and fish that, Swedish meatballs and noodles, all the Swedes and us, Dr. Willard Johnson, and what was his wife's name, Julia Johnson, this over-sexed cutie pie with the ample tits and upswept hair who ended up getting "allergic" to Willard and getting a divorce and marrying another member, Ollie Olson for all I remember.

Sometimes we'd bring my grandmother over to the club and she'd go into the slot-machine room (only allowed in private clubs back then) and she'd wait around, watch someone put fifty quarters in a machine with no results, and then she'd go over and put in two quarters, and, bingo, a jackpot.

Everyone knew her.

"Hello, Mrs. Mangan."

Mrs. Mangan this, Mrs. Mangan that.

She had a winning way with her, always a little smile, a quip.

I hate to say it, but like all the old Jewish ladies over at the temple that I know. Never at a loss for words.

We'd go down to Kungsholm a lot. Downtown Chicago.

More smorgasboard, more cold/smoked fish. And full-length operas like Wagner's Tristan and Isolde or the Ring operas, *Siefried, Die Gotterdammerung.* Especially the Ring operas, all about Norse (almost Swedish) myth.

But we never got really close with the Swedes. We were close to the Greimans, OK, to Fanny and Doctor Morris, all that vast army of Jewish watch makers and jewelers and furriers and tailors that surrounded us.

My mother was right out of the movies, that poor, beautiful bitch who wants to make it big and get inside the American dream, get the big house, the big car, big house, fur coats and diamond watches and earrings.

She was a real beauty, and every time I went to a Bette Davis or Joan Crawford or Lana Turner film, there she was up on the screen, seductive, hungry, full of fire and neuroses, wanting to put her shadey past behind her and enter triumphant into the WASP world, still managing, though, to somehow accept her Irish side, her Irish relatives . . . although even there the concentration was on the Anglo side of the Irishers: "The Kirbys were from England, not from Ireland at all." As if the name Kirby wasn't Irish.

At the same time there was this endless flirtation with everything Jewish, and when I came back from Brazil in 1978 with long hair and I went to visit her in Mount St. Antonio Gardens, where she'd moved after my father had died, she took one look at my long hair and said "How can you wear a kipu with that kind of hair?"

You know, a kipu, the skullcaps that Jewish men wear during services.

"What do you know about kipus?" I asked her.

"I know everything there is to know," she answered, then kind of wished she hadn't.

Everything there is to know about kipus. And, I suspect, everything else Jewish. It was there, it was her, her whole life was one long denial of what she really was.

Which cheated me out of all kinds of "richness," didn't it?

I learned some Latin, of course, but what if I'd learned Hebrew?

When I finally did learn it fifty years later, and one of my Israeli students gave me a chart of comparative ancient semitic scripts from one of the museums in Jerusalem and I started looking at the different kinds of ancient alphabets, about a year later I began to see the writing on two thousand year old pots of the Mochica Indians in Peru and slowly began to realize that all the drawings on the vast number of Mochica pots that have come down to us all portray Hercules myths. The Mochica Indians were Phoenicians. The writing was Phoenician. Something I never would have discovered if I hadn't studied Hebrew.

Not to mention all the personal bonding I missed, the contact with all the old Jews in my grandmother's family, belonging to the tribe, learning what it was to be a mensch, all the hands touched, the reassurances, the tribal sense that breaks the horrible feeling of loneliness that pursues tiny man on this vast earth in the middle of the even more vast skies.

I was robbed, cheated, swindled. I wish I could go back now and open a door and walk into a Passover seder at my great-grandfather's and great-stepmother's, surrounded by great-aunts and uncles, aunts and uncles, break a little bread, drink a little wine, feel that deep, warm, essential love that says THIS IS WHO YOU ARE, THIS IS WHERE YOU FOREVER BELONG . . . .

It was bad enough to be a brotherless and sisterless only child. But to take away my Jewish inheritance. Why? Because the old black-hatted, long-haired, Yiddish-speaking tribe wasn't good enough for Madame Helen!

Summers at a YMCA camp in Delevan, Wisconsin or at Bloom's Turkey Farm in Chesterton, Indiana or with my grandmother in Cicero when I was very young, before she'd lost her house. And then later my father would get me jobs with his patients. Ed O'Malley and the O'Malley Construction Company. Digging ditches. Or there was a Mr. Sorenson, a cook for the Fred Harvey Service at the Santa Fe Railroad. A job as a chicken butcher, all day all summer in the deep freeze cutting up chickens, or when I was out of the freezer I'd be cutting up livers or steaks, blood all over my clothes, no way to avoid it and I'd come out and get on the bus and everyone would move away from me. Imagine Chicago at a super-humid 95 degrees, and me stinking of chicken fit and beef blood.

Get rid of me as much as possible.

Get rid of that fucker, Hugh, so we can have a little fun around here.

It was part of that whole 30's-40's image of The Bitch, poor, outide, close to her immigrant background, dying to get inside The American Scene. Outsider to Insider. And the only way to get there was with what she had between her legs. And the legs themselves, always carefully clad in the silkiest possible stockings, garter belts, spongy, mostly black underthings, lacey bras, beautifully shaped breasts. That was a good idea to have one kid for, wasn't it? Just to build up your breasts.

All my mother's big whore lingerie wasn't for fun but action . . . lots of it. The lingerie and the shoes and the endless diamond rings and watches that she was always buying. What was the name of the jeweler downtown, Mr. Siegel? I was there so often that I felt like he was an old friend.

It was funny when we'd go to a Christmas party at one of my father's sister's houses, like Aunt Babe's. There would be Aunt Elsie, short, pudgy, a high school Spanish teacher (Harrison High School), an old spinster who had gotten all her father's fortune, Aunt Pearl and her five kids, my five cousins, her husband Jack Fewkes, a high school football coach, also head of the Chicago Teacher's Union, and then Aunt Babe (Margeret) herself, with her three kids, Bobby, Georgy and Margie. They'd all be OK, dressed up like normal. And my mother would appear on the scene like a combination of Gretta Garbo, Gloria Swanson and Hedy Lamarr. She never walked but strutted, like she was out on a fashion runway, never talked, but giggled, screamed, laughed, played coy, always the queen, the superior, always like she was coming into Grauman's Chinese Theater to get an Academy Award for the Cheapest Trick of the Year.

She should have gone into Medicine herself instead of riding my father's degree all her life. She was brainy and energetic, and all of it got funnelled into vanity and sex. One thing my father was, was sexually satisfied, that was for sure.

"Go visit your grandmother," my mother would say come nightfall . . .

Hugh Fox is an icon of twentieth century American literature. Born in 1932, he immersed himself in music and art at an early age, encouraged by his parents, a violinist-turned-M.D. and a frustrated actress. Three years of pre-med led to a B.S. in Humanities and an M.A. in English from Loyola University in Chicago. After traveling in Europe, Fox earned a Ph.D. in American Literature from the University of Illinois at Urbana-Champaign, then became a professor American Literature in Los Angeles. Later he moved to the Department of American Thought and Language at Michigan State University, where he is an emeritus professor. Fox has traveled and taught extensively in Latin America and lectured in Spain and Portugal. Charles Bukowski's first critical biographer, his own poems are legion and legendary, as is his fiction. His novel *Shaman* has been ranked with *On the Road*. In addition, Fox is well known as an editor of avant garde literary magazines. According to *Poets' Encyclopedia*, "Hugh Fox has eighty-five books published, and another thirty (mainly novels, plays and one archaeology book) still on the shelves." He currently lives with his Brazilian-born wife in Lansing, Michigan, and is writing.

Carol Novack

Cluck Cluck

being my mini-memoir for readings
at which everyone but my two friends
is younger than thirty-two
(for Raymond Federman)

On the road

She's pushing 50 plus, don't ask. No more Southern Comfort orgies, existential funhouse trips, Kundalini embraces in grottos, poetry benders, and slightly protected sex, she's busy trying to be the heroine of the story, a third person.

But I wasn't sold on third person, so I asked you, Mickey, *should I speak in the first person, tell the story as if I had lived it?* You'd just finished an MFA program in creative writing. You knew everything. The glass over your displayed stamped degree was fresh. Already, you were teaching Oates and Boyle wannabes about arcs and resolutions. I asked you, *novel or something vaguely biographical?* You said: *Write a memoir. Put your life in the first person. Make it up if you can't remember it make it shocking or pathetic but don't tell anyone and above all, make people laugh hard and weep easily. Look in the display windows at Barnes and Nobles. It's all about memoir, displays of courage amidst adversity. It's about people overcoming, surviving all sorts of shit. I know you can do it*, you said, *I know an agent.* You were licking your lips when you said that. You and your 20 and 30 something MFA friends were drinking Michelob. You're still drinking. I see you in the audience, little bro. I should learn from you, selling your first novel to Random House.

She was pulling more than 50 years after her. Distillization, even on a modest scale, seemed daunting. Heaps of shit to recount and re-invent. *Yes it's overwhelming*, I said to you, *but one must try, I understand, I am told.* Your wan, bulimic girlfriend with the belly button ring was in the kitchen fixing something like Vegan tofutti with soy cheese; her skin was blinking like strobe lights. Must've been glitter. My skin is dry with furrows like clay from the Paleolithic Age. I was trying a new skin cream from Aveda at the time, I think. Now it's "facial sculpting" cream by some company owned by a dermatologist in New York. Your girlfriend Zappa drinks bottled water, 12 Evians per day. She'll never run dry until the mother of all tsunamis comes along to get all of us who are still alive. The Greenland icebergs are sagging, falling flat into the ocean up there, like dead breasts. Time to leave coastal areas.

So as I was saying to all of you dear young things, she the older woman was somewhere I forget. Already I've misplaced her, losing my memory and hers in tandem. At least, I should give her a name. I was considerate enough to give you and your girlfriend names. How about Melanoma? Okay okay, I'm kidding, nothing to joke about, stop jumping up and down and screaming. You've been trying to make me see this or that ever since you could formulate sentences. You with the cherub cheeks, Kirk Douglas dent in your chin, from the maternal grandfather, always wearing your hair so short nobody like me would ever want to run her fingers through it. Good idea. Keep me at a distance.

This is getting complicated psychologically and I only have so much time, she thought. I can't possibly go everywhere in one story. I'll look for somewhere to start. Which reminds me of a chicken.

Why did the chicken refuse to cross the road? Take those i-pods off, please please, birdbrains. Focus your eyes and take something to clear your sinuses. The traffic is belching like a behemoth with botulism, choking on fumes from a caravan of SUV's, slouching toward Orlando and Miami, palm trees and parking lots under a navel orange smiley face. Would you cross a road under these circumstances? Look at the drivers with their cellular pacifiers. They are everywhere but here, you know. The solipsists would run you down and scamper off with their lawyers. *Mommy, mommy — — I want to see Poo-poo the Penguin!* Didn't you cry when Mickey Mouse died? Oh, you didn't know?

So Melanoma okay Melody sat on the curb of a road that winds like a tapeworm from west to east or east to west, depending on who's telling the story. So maybe she's in Missouri, where I've never been. I need to consult my friend Alla in St. Louis. Hang on. Okay, I can dance the Google too! Seems the road starts down there somewhere, but it's hard to follow and I can't get in touch with Alla who's in Orlando with the boys I just recalled.

Melody was bereft, tuneless. *Bereft of what? And what's her song?* you ask. Too many facocta questions for nothing, no reason. Why questions? *Knock it off,* I say, I've always been bereft of my senses, according to many. *Stop being hyperbolic*, you said dramatically. I think it's a love song by that Hebrew hater Wagner . . . . Liebe strom-untdrung something whatever. Au secours! Courage, mes enfants! *Awesome! Wunderbar! Chocolat!* She also likes that Nancy Sinatra song about walking boots.

So where was I? On the curb, the stingy, gritty curb of existence, hard on the ass, as usual on the rim of it all, the ledge of success, well to tell the truth far from the ledge but about to fall off, floating on the circumference of meaning, riding a cycle around my self, skirting it in my pink pantaloons with white satin ribbons. *Huh? pantaloons? Where did you get them?* You asked. You said: *too many images confuse me and when you add abstractions, you totally lose it, you know you lose us. You're like a planet in another solar system called Chaos. You don't follow the rules and you're much too self-indulgent to get anywhere*, you said. You were emulating the minimalists, as you'd been taught to do. You accused me of swimming unconsciously in streams of consciousness, told me I'm passe with an accent. May a tsunami weep over you, I didn't say, being somewhat mature. I realized you were upset with me. You usually never simile! But I digress of necessity, as necessity invents digression and digression is the mother of invention.

There were very essential pantaloons in my past, in Melanoma's history, they suddenly bloom large enough to see hanging on a clothesline in the backyard of a vine-choked stone house in Funafuti, the capitol of the isles of Tuvalu, in which I'll dwell circa 2019, pantaloons hanging as symbols of the teenage girl's coming of age in the early 60's, past the hoola hoop stage, at one of those times (during the last century) when girls who'd teetered over the edge of puberty twittered about wedding nights, wondering what they'd wear to bed and oh wow, what would *he* feel like, Before i-pods and all that techno stuff kids think they can't live without. Do girls still do that? Melody wondered, particularly girls with pins in their tongues and tattoos of stars on their breasts?

So pantaloons are important in my mini-memoir I think, Melanoma insisted. The heat was loud that Sunday. Flat, hopeful voices singing dour hymns wafted futilely across the landscape of corn and wheat. No, not both, you boob. Choose. And don't use all of those adjectives and adverbs! Okay, corn, though this wasn't Iowa. It was (as understood) uncomfortable on the curb and the donkey was panting. Yes, the donkey, she always shows up (footnote: *e.g.,* see Novack's "Interview with Self"), the ass drops by. She had an ass, always did, came by it naturally, naturally. It was drooping from the burdens of years of sitting on itself. Asses don't last. You will learn. Okay, you and Raymond Federman mistrust metaphors. I can't help it they drop by without even ringing bells. Should I call the cops?

Melody lusted suddenly for King Kong the supermarket of all supermarkets. Henry had insisted she acquire a cell phone so she could consult him while she shopped. *Okay, Henry,* she would say into the phone. *I'm by the carrots. Do you want any? No? Oh please, not okra. You know I loathe okra! . . . . So now I'm by the fish and there are some elegant yet tragic baby octopuses, fresh from Santorini, glistening with Greek salt shine, even.* And Henry would reply with incredulity: *What the fuck, are you kidding? Yuck!*

I was nearing a coma from the heat. I'd left the Bombay gin behind, of necessity, having fled with startling alacrity. The cops. They would find all of us under the beds with our leaflets. I'd had it with Henry anyway. Had IT, if you know what I mean or even if you don't, this is gritty realism. This memoir is authentic and exciting, full of tragedies. But talking about failed relationships is boring, at my age, at least. Being 20 something, maybe you think I can teach you something. Forget it. You couldn't take my life, take it and make something of it, like a lesson in perseverance. You wouldn't know what to do with it. It's much too messy, you'd say. Knowing you, you'd reduce it drastically, deleting the most succulent bits, like those references to creme brulee, fatty pastrami, pistachio nuts, and long boned loin lamb chops. Now Melody forgets even what Henry looked like though he was everything to her, the sun, the moon, the stars, the big screen television and especially the waterbed, particularly when it leaked, threatening instant death by electric shock. Once they flowed together, bounced in harmony to the beat of some band or other. He was meaningful.

Sitting on the curb with my fat ass. We were both thirsty and there was no grass left. So you want I should suddenly have a realization that will change my life or something dramatic should happen. Well it did. A big white SUV with LALA plates rear-ends my ass and takes off, tires squealing, gas fuming. Dang dang, no fuckin transportation now. *That's silly*, you say. *But where was Melody going?*

Melody was seeking her next song, the one after Henry, who was always the same chords, the same beat outside the bedrooms. She was delirious from the sun, a mass of discordant notes and hair, aimless. Nobody ever listened to her. She would often say: You're not LISTENING. And she would frequently get no response, frequently because she'd forgotten to open her mouth to utter her questions. *I want to make a difference*, I would often say. And you would ask suspiciously, *a difference in what? To what? How different?* Jeez, you gave me headaches, always did, as if you were listening, which you weren't. You were always too busy. Always. Hang on. That's someone else's American father I'm remembering.

But that's no matter. I see this guy up the road, let's say a lat-ish 40'ish dish full of sinews, trying to hitch a ride. Nobody picks up hikers you should know, no longer, after Ted Bundy. Nobody refers to a guy as a dish. This guy is waving four signs at the passing vehicles. One of them says: IS ANYONE GOING TO TENNESSEE? Another states: FORMER LINGUISTICS PROFESSOR NEEDS RIDE TO TALLAHASSEE. The third sign reads: ANYWHERE WILL DO. And the fourth sign asks: HOW ABOUT SASKATEWAN?

On this road, everyone's going east. The former professor imagines that he has a choice. Melody finds that endearing.

You will go anywhere, anywhere but here. Understood. I know that. In that, we are alike. Melody will go anywhere. She wants to overcome everything by walking away, riding donkeys, getting ON with her life, getting unstuck from the same rhythms and notes.

So why a former linguistics professor? You ask.

He'd had enough of the language of uttered and written words. He wanted to carve mountains out of molehills, I reply. *That's the answer, I can't help it*, I add, walking into the closet.

In the truck

I make miracles. The professor and I are finding ourselves in a truck going west. The sun is mellowing and we're drinking tequila and we're so friggin happy we're not going to Florida. *It's all about love you know*, mother said forgetting all the shit all about love and songs, *All you need is love,* so it's inevitable he and I are in the truck together, sitting so close in the front seat our thighs are touching, I can feel his warmth and that old familiar ache and ripple in my nether regions. That's where she's at that woman, 19 years old in a long hippy dress, remembering her mother in one of mother's irrational wistful moods. Here's Melody with crazy red-headed jazzman Don riding in a banged up VW all the way to New York City from Rochester, New York, Don being nothing but a brilliant sloppy trippy boozer without his piano, drinking Southern Comfort and popping LSD all the way. It's a wonder she survived. In her last year of college she's persistently overcoming an urge to drop out and off the ledge. So in love with older what's his name who never calls. Lived in The Village and looked like Trevor Howard, that guy. I was overcome and his name was David. I think he's still in Alaska. Ah.

Where were we? Oh now, Don, he's real, overcame booze and runs an auto repair shop somewhere in the southwest, I know where, but I'm not telling. He was always good with cars he didn't wreck.

I digress.

You want to know what happens next and before next. You want some deaths, rapes and divorces. Okay, so you were wild during your college years, to be expected. *Get on with it*, you urge. You want to know what happens with the linguistics professor and what he has to do with overcoming adversities and also adversaries when Melody was a lawyer championing underdogs usually shit poor and fucked up on drugs, other times on art. But this is a mere soupcon of a life in progression and regression I am offering you, take it or leave it. You forget, you young things. Don and Henry and David and that professor are all parts of it. Two of them are real perhaps. Melody gets them mixed up now, fatally ill after a suicide attempt.

What? Wait just a minute! you say. *You're jumping the gun, aren't you? And this doesn't sound like a memoir. I don't believe any of this*, you say, starting to walk away. *You're having me on, mocking me. I'm off to Barnes & Noble.*

Then I will narrate my mini-memoir without you. See if I care! My memory moves selectively without me, offering images of pain and pleasure, no more no less. You can put them together and make a quilt. That's not my job. I will pick out what interests me, on a fluke, on the lamb, what occurs to me as I think about Melody's life. There is Melody with Don, Melody with Henry, Melody with David and Melody with the former linguistics professor. At one point there is Melody with Jeffrey and at another, Melody with Norman, but I'm not getting into Norman in particular, no never. Nobody ever did and he disappeared in Cairo years ago anyway.

I already told you about the pantaloons. Melody is a self-deluding woman who's imagined loving many men. If she were a man, perhaps she'd describe cars she has loved. Unconditionally. Don't ask me. Once in a while, she thinks of her Buffet clarinet and the sounds the Atlantic Ocean makes when nobody's listening. Also the old people on the boardwalk. Did I mention she grew up within kissing distance of the ocean and played a clarinet? Is that important?

Okay, okay, teach us something about love, you ask. *Please continue.*

Melody is in the truck with the professor and they're having a terrific time of it; she's never met such a man, vibrant, wise, warm, melancholy and whimsical. And then he gets out, at some exit I forget which, somewhere in Oklahoma I think. That's the most I can remember about the affair. Oh, wait a sec: once the driver got out to pee and the professor bit me on my right tit. Well of course, that was the one closest to him, you boobs!

You're not happy. *Oh come on,* you say. *You made that up. You keep leaving us stranded, without a story — there's nothing satisfying about any of this!*

I apologize. Sometimes life has a way of running out of steam. Sometimes you think big things like proms and graduations and earth-shattering insights are happening and then when you're not looking the big things evaporate. Even to remember them would take effort. Sometimes we remember things like finding bees in our pockets. Okay. I admit that I remember that, I *own* it, as the social workers would say. I own that a bee stung me when I put my hand in my pocket, sacrificing its life to teach me a lesson in morality. The bee flew into my pocket to punish me for being mean to a poor girl named Gail I think, though I can't be sure and I don't remember what she looked like. No, you're right. Her name wasn't Gail. That was someone else I knew at another time.

And did you overcome your guilt? You ask.

Melody says *never. Every time I'm mean to someone, a bee flies into my heart and stings it. When I die under mysterious circumstances, the coroner will find a mass of dead bees where my heart should've been.*

Sometimes there's simply a story that moves cyclically from progression to digression to regression to progression to digression and so on, stopping along the way to eat grass. It could start with a question about a chicken and you could put an ass in it, but people would expect the ass to push the story forward. Every detail must push the story forward to its denouement and there is no story without a denouement. That's what they say. *Asses pull. They don't push,* you insist, audibly annoyed.

Melody's ass has always done things ass backwards, I respond. *That's educational!*

In the kitchen

Why are we now in a kitchen? You ask. You want to know what happened to the chicken. That's why. You complain about the unfinished and underdone story of the chicken, but don't you realize that one comes across so many chickens during the course of one's life? For all you know that chicken is the one in the pot with the carrots and celery and dill and onions and of course garlic. *Don't be ridiculous,* you say. *The chicken in the pot can't be the same chicken that refused to cross the road. That was in another place at another time,* you say with certainty. *There you go being positive,* I respond.

Raymond Federman thinks that chicken on the curb of the road should've met its demise at the wheels of an SUV as the chicken was trying to get to the other side. That would be logical because chickens are notorious birdbrains, but I didn't have the heart to push the chicken into the road. How would you like to see a living creature mangled? You think I should contribute to road kill, even in a story, even worse in a mini-memoir? Should I sacrifice a chicken to an SUV as a political statement? Should I reduce a chicken to a metaphor? That was one smart chicken, a rare chicken who knew that the other side of the road held no promises. You want displays of courage in memoirs, so I gave you one: a chicken that acted out of character. Melody won't quibble. She stopped paying attention to the chicken when she noticed the former linguistics professor. Between the chicken and the professor, the focal point was the ass.

Melody won't talk about her father's death. She can't do it and she can't overcome it. But I digress. As if I were progressing. Where were we?

Focus, kiddies. Turn off those technological attachments. We are all in the kitchen and you want to know what happened to Melody after we left the professor somewhere in Oklahoma, maybe. *We?* You ask. You pout. Well okay, to be precise, I left him somewhere or he left me somewhere. He was a fragment of story, no more, no less. Sorry to be blunt, but some people are Buddhists, so they'll understand it's silly to hang onto either a man or a chicken. I've passed Oklahoma, if that was where he went off on his own. Melody ended up in this kitchen at some point. From Oklahoma to the kitchen or the kitchen to Oklahoma or maybe Missouri to New York and back to Saskatewan and then to the kitchen, no matter. The smells of the chicken cooking overcome such concerns. *Cut the chicken,* you say.

You persist. *We want to know how Melody continued without the linguistics professor, what affects his departure had on her, whether he left a wound that hasn't healed, whether she lost hope forever, after that did she meet another man or found a school for women without linguistic professors?*

Every man that leaves a woman leaves a vacancy in her life, I answered. And it is the same for men when women leave them. So he left a vacancy of which I was unaware, a vacancy another man couldn't possibly fill. The same goes for close relatives. We are so full of vacancies, all of us. Know that. It's important. *Are you crying yet? Am I moving you yet, you silly putty? You want to know about my father's death? Forget it.*

Melody is in the kitchen feeling vacant, chewing on tender chicken bones, and persistently overcoming adversity whether she knows it or not. She thinks that a long time ago many of her ancestors in Ukrainian villages were murdered by Cossacks. She thinks how lucky she is that she wasn't in Germany during the Nazi years or in Russia when Jews in villages were routinely murdered. So she thinks there's little to overcome when you haven't been victimized severely by historical circumstances (including hurricanes and tsunamis), mistreated horrifically as a child or stricken by severe diseases.

Melody thinks that sometimes one must overcome adversity by refusing to do what people expect you to do. So when doctors say you have an incurable disease but you'll live for six more months if you die quietly in a hospice and eat porridge, kale, and bananas, you say no way, go on a trip to Madagascar, and eat fried meat with fried rice and hot peppers. Instead of marrying a suave, handsome linguistics professor (no, not necessarily *that* one) who makes you swoon in bed, you marry his gauche, impecunious cousin because he's brilliant and makes you laugh and then you divorce him because he's neurotic as hell and really hates his mother whom he never overcame so he's passive-aggressive and does all sorts of things to pain you.

Melody's former best friend Francine says one must overcome adversity by finding a feminist therapist and learning how to kill one's father and all those abusive men who resembled him and one can only do this by writing one's memoirs and getting them published by Random House. On the other hand, Annette says she overcame early childhood and adolescent abuse by entering an ashram in India with a guru originally from the Bronx, who was great at oral sex. Marc says that Annette must've been reading Updike's "S."

So okay, I'm at the end of my mini-memoir. You are tired of Melody because she has set no example. There are so many words I can waste on a life that holds no vision of a best seller type of overcoming, a life that merely climbs, reclines, and declines in turns, stumbles on and on, like that ass. We all end up in a kitchen, more or less, because obviously we all have to eat and really those of us who have kitchens are very lucky, so keep sucking on those Michelob nipples and pass the Sweet-and-Low.

Carol Novack says: "There is a long distance to travel back and so much extraneous extravaganza, I think I have lost most parts on the way, forget where the tale of this life lies, the fortunes and misses, miss what is left, if anything, suspect I may be invisible in the mirrors, may have already misplaced myself, mistaking my self for a metaphor, may or may have, forget . . . Read *Giraffes in Hiding: The Mythical Memoirs of Carol Novack* (spuytenduyvil.net); carol-novack.blogspot.com."

Jim Chaffee

Noise in the Machine:
The Homogeneous Chaos Blues
(for Roger Carlson)

Gilbert Ryle nailed Cartesian dualism by killing the ghost in the machine. Now someone named Carl Zimmer wants to use noise in the machine to kill a straw man standing in for genetic determinism. This mushy-headed blather arises as an attempt to simulate science-talk to people inured to comic book encapsulation of the most complex ideas. Who knows what the author intended to convey, or why, but the premise demands deconstruction like Lon Cheney Junior demanded a dew claw.

I don't know squat about Zimmer, having run across this article in a roundabout manner. A Brazilian in an Orkut community opened a topic with the heading "Fim do determinismo genetico." He posted a link to a Portuguese translation of an article appearing in a Brazilian online newspaper. [1]

Intrigued, I went to the link and began as I usually do, reading the opening sentence claiming that humans differ from one another in an infinity of aspects. It made me hope there had been a mistranslation. No respectable science writer would claim the existence of an actual infinity of physical anythings (though it isn't clear aspects need be physical).

This led me to look for the original source from The New York Times, which I found online, dated April 22, 2008. [2] The author wrote that humans differ in too many ways to count, which is a far cry from differing in an infinity of aspects.

The original essay is entitled "Expressing Our Individuality, the Way E. Coli Do." Catchy, no? Were it not already penned, I'd have to invent it.

If you take the time to read this short bit, the straw man pops right up into your headlights, assuming you have them on. Otherwise you might miss him, disguised as he is: Zimmer contends we put a bigger premium on nature than nurture when it comes to our individuality. I'm not sure where he gets this idea, unless its his own *welt-*

anschauung. It's not mine.

Nor is it the view I ever run across, excepting the bizarre commercial that instructs me I get my cholesterol from my aunt. Most of the people I know believe that when they get a disease or condition it's their own fault, usually dietary, and not that of their genes. They like to feel in control, I think. Sort of the inverse of conspiracy theory or Existentialism as substitute for God.

As you read along you find this Zimmer trying to convince you that you think bacteria like E. coli (proper name Escherichia) are machines. Which is amusing. The only human I know of who said any kind of animals (I'm loosening the notion of animal here) were machines was Rene Descartes, who Bertrand Russell claimed didn't believe it but wanted to avoid the physical duress of the Inquisition's enforced insistence that humans were the only souled creatures. Another kind of ghost in the not-machine, so to speak.

I personally would have been surprised if all bacteria in a colony behaved alike, or that the behavior was predictable. But that is not the most interesting aspect of what Zimmer writes. After informing us that bacteria "are not simple machines," he brings in the idea of noise changing the way the E. coli bacteria behave. He says that unlike transistors and wires, "E. coli molecules are floppy, twitchy and unpredictable." This he contrasts to the deterministic behavior of electronic devices.

So right off the bat here, Zimmer misrepresents electronic devices in the way that Descartes misrepresented animals, though my guess is Zimmer did it for money and not fear of torture (he might simply be ignorant). Anyone who has worked with electronic gizmos on spacecraft will have experienced these mechanisms getting out of hand. In the early days of GPS when the satellites disappeared from view for a few hours, on-board atomic clocks might decide to leap in time. When they reappeared they would be so far off that the Kalman filter at the Master Control Station could be falsely persuaded by new measurements that the satellite had hopped to a lunar orbit.

Even more interesting is metastability in certain binary electronic devices known as flip-flops. With only two possible states, the device can become confused and take an indeterminate (random) time to decide whether to flip or flop.

And who is the culprit for these and too many other aspects of electronic misbehavior to count?

Noise, as it turns out. Which is in fact like a weed. That is, akin to the chicory in my garden that is currently out of hand, inedible and blooming and propagating even as I continually pull it up all summer so other plants can grow. But is it a weed? Not in the winter, when the leaves darken red and purple to become radicchio.

Noise is a random process, a not well-defined thingy in the real world from what I can gather. Random processes do have precise mathematical meaning, however fraught with difficulties in the quotidian world swept under the rug of operational definition. If you doubt the difficulties, read chapters two and four of Leo Breiman's classic text *Probability*. Or at least the discussion at the end of the chapters, though the discourse on conditional probability is particularly mind-bending.

Here is the real deal. It seems the "real world" we live in is a world of aggregates: averages of random stuff at the microscopic level. At least that seems to be the world according to quantum theory. Or statistical mechanics. So to say that electronic or mechanical or electro-mechanical devices behave at the atomic level like machines, that is mechanistically, is specious.

The examples cited above (and numerous others) provide counterexamples to Zimmer's quasi-example, at least as represented. E. coli behaves oddly at the macroscopic level because it is not predictable at the microscopic level, even given identical genes and identical situations. Well, there is a problem with that identical situation bit, since it is not clear there is ever any identical situation. But just as E. coli get trapped in various deviant feedback loops and other aberrant behavior, so can electronic devices. And not predictably, though one might try to replicate a situation exactly.

In fact with noise the idea of replication is fraught with difficulty. In a computer simulation it is possible to use a pseudo-random number generator and begin it with the same seed, getting the exact same pseudo-random sequence of numbers (which is why it is not a random number generator). However, the simulation is not the device itself. This point has been well demonstrated by John Searle in regards to the problem of consciousness in strong artificial intelligence, wherein he points out that the idea of a machine that simulates consciousness is not equivalent to the machine being conscious. Consciousness, argues the materialist Searle, is a physical process akin to digestion, and simulating digestion is not digesting (but consider for argument sake Wim Delvoye's Cloaca). And pseudo-random noise in a software-controlled machine is not random noise in a software-controlled machine.

The mathematical idea of random process is not likely what an engineer might imagine in any case. The idea is that the manifestation is not itself random, but is in fact determined. What is random is the picking of that particular manifestation. As if some infinite dice roll hands us the result. Of course, not being privy to the outcome beforehand, we must contend with the manifestation as if it itself unfolded randomly in time.

So where are we? Starting with an attempt to befuddle us by claiming we confuse phenotype with genotype, we end up with the claim that bacteria are different from machines because of noise. More sleight of hand, it seems, illustrated in the essay's conclusion: "Living things are more than just programs run by genetic software."

And yet electronic machines run by software can become confused as to whether an input is yes or no. (There was a time when engineers believed such behavior from a digital device to be impossible, causing all manner of difficulty in searching for a non-existent software bug, another kind of ghost in the machine.) And noise is the culprit.

The classical feedback-loop known as the phase-locked loop, essential for tracking signals in all sorts of radios and myriad other electronic devices, can suffer all manner of unspeakably unpredictable behavior with noise, from the audible clicks of cycle-slips in FM radio to false lock. More complex types of software feedback loops like the extended Kalman filter can become so confused they eventually insist on the spurious, divergence sometimes termed instability, driving the machines they control to irrational behavior. (The honest-to-God Kalman filter under certain circumstance cannot (in the long run) tell a lie, a condition known as stability.) What is more, the phase-locked loop has been taken as a model for the behavior of living cells.

The real issue, it seems, is not machine versus living thing, but determinism versus randomness.

It brings to mind (the word only a metaphor, but for what?) a conversation with an engineer some years ago. Not a unique conversation, to be sure, because the idea she expressed is common. She said that nothing was ever random. If you knew all the initial conditions and all the forces in a coin toss, for example, you would be able to tell exactly how the coin would land. I replied that was a metaphysical assumption and could not be demonstrated experimentally. Much of the discussion above goes to the heart of showing that such an argument is metaphysical, not physical. It is a metaphysical ideology known as determinism.

To be sure, all evidence of which I am aware is contrary to determinism. No matter how careful a calculation is made, for example, the implementation always misses the mark. Approximate cause and effect seems the nub of perceived determinism. But let's see why causality is probably (in what sense here this word?) not demonstrable.

If I smash a plate with a hammer, I demonstrate a cause and its effect. Determinism at work: the hammer smashes the plate. Right? But what if I hit exactly the same plate, with exactly the same hammer, in exactly the same way again? Would the plate break into the same exact pieces? No one can say. There's the rub. If this cannot be repeated, then it cannot be predicted, and thus is not what could be called deterministic. Hence not really cause and effect except via the fog of imprecision; that is, so long as one doesn't look too closely.

In order to ascertain if this particular event is truly determined, in the sense that given the precise initial conditions one can exactly predict the outcome at whatever level one examines, one might decide to repeat the experiment. If we cannot ever know all the initial conditions, we ought still be able, by repeating the precise experiment, to get precisely the same outcome in a deterministic world.

But how can we repeat this experiment?

Suppose I build a machine to precisely smash a plate placed in precise position, a plate made of precisely the same materials in precisely the same way as its predecessor.

You could argue, This is not the same experiment. What are pieces exactly the same? At what level? Molecular? Atomic? Subatomic? Is it possible to use the same exact hammer again, given that it had already smashed a plate? Is it possible to construct the exact same plate? In fact, would that original plate be the same exact plate a fractional step later? That is, if I smashed the plate a picosecond later would I be smashing the same plate that had existed a picosecond earlier? On a macro enough level, certainly. But do the micro properties make a difference even in this temporally loaded case?

This argument is along the lines of the famous saying of Heraclitus to the effect that one cannot step into the same river twice. Nothing new here. (Actually, we stand before a crossroad with a branch leading to questions of dependence on initial conditions, stability, and chaos theory, but we forgo the fork since it would take us too far afield. Suffice it to say the chaos of chaos theory is not random behavior, though it might appear so to the untrained eye. But look to Smale's horseshoe!)

The question I am putting is, if it were possible to exactly replicate the experiment, would the results be the same?

I see no reason to believe so. I foresee noise fucking things up, changing the outcome ever so slightly. Perhaps only detectable at microscopic level, but still and all different.

So what the hell is deterministic, anyway? Well, it isn't the opposite of random, that's for damned sure.

Deterministic is if you start at some place with specified conditions, you will without fail end up at a place at a later time that can be precisely predicted without deviation. You follow a trajectory, if you will, not in the sense of bogus-speak [3] as demonstrated by Petraeus and Crocker, but a trajectory in the sense of mechanics. Traditionally, determinism is behavior obtained from differential equations, be they ordinary or partial. The idea is that starting from some initial conditions, like the position and velocity of my hammer, the outcome is completely known once the differential equation describing the hammer blow is known.

As parenthetically hinted above, there is oversimplification here due in part to my own desire to avoid the complication of chaos and the confusion of chaotic bopping for randomness. The little book *Chaotic Evolution and Strange Attractors* by David Ruelle is a lovely side excursion if you have the time and fuel for it, with a mathematical description of a chaotic information-creating machine. (Akin to an information Cloaca?) However, for our purposes let's pretend to be happy Taoists following the trajectory of the wise man, avoiding struggle as we go with the flow, so to speak (flow in the precise sense).

Noise is a random process, and randomness is not the opposite of determinism. Already we've alluded to as much above, discussing noise at the micro level averaging up to what we experience at the macro level, the quasi-regularity engineers love to extrapolate to determinism fucked by imperfect information. This seems to be perhaps Ruelle's viewpoint, though I am not certain. (There are those who attempt to explain away noise by equating it with chaotic behavior and lack of information as part and parcel of the metaphysical assumption of determinism.) But random behavior is controlled by laws that allow predictions in the long run; of course, as Keynes noted, in the long run we're all dead.

If you're still along, grab a padded, well-secured seat and clutch something substantial. We face a wild-ass ride coming right up, so irregular it will shake loose anything not bolted down. Can't be helped, but you might like it. An honest-to-God Coney Island of the mind, so to speak.

In 1827, English botanist Robert Brown noted peculiar behavior of small particles suspended in fluid. They were, it seems, floppy, twitchy and unpredictable. This jitterbug waltz gained the title Brownian motion. And though this erraticism came to be considered a manifestation of molecular motion, it wasn't until 1905 that Albert Einstein invented a suitable theory. Said kinetic theory got itself amended in the physical world later, since Einstein's own explanation was not completely satisfactory, leading to infractions of one or two laws of nature. The fun part came, however, not from any considerations of natural-law abiding physicists but from lawless mathematicians, beginning with Norbert Wiener.

Norbert ran with this illegal idea and created from it a fantastical creature representing Einstein's logically wanting physical theory.

(This academic behavior is a source of irritation to physicists who cannot understand why it is necessary to create an elaborate ruse to make logically inconsistent ideas meet the rigor demanded by the mathematical artist. The most famous example might be Paul Dirac and Laurent Schwartz. Perhaps Emerson's phrase consistency is the hobgoblin of little minds ought be the motto of physicists.) What Norbert created lived in an infinite dimensional space of functions, and was indeed a way of measuring chunks of such large places, albeit in a rather roundabout way for the likes of most of us. He gave it names like the homogeneous chaos (which has nothing to do with the chaos alluded to above, and in fact predates it by half a century more or less), and his process came to be known as the Wiener process, though a lot of mathematicians still call it Brownian motion, being dubious of, or at least unconcerned with, physical reality.

And Norbert made the engineer's white noise a living mathematical fiction via his construction of Brownian motion.

Literary types love terms like white noise, though they seldom have a pig's-eye view of what the hell it is. To be somewhat carelessly careful, white noise is a random process wherein events are independent of one another, no matter how close together they may occur in time. In other words, if you see what this guy did at some time, you will have no idea what it will do "next" or any time later. The white noise immediately forgets where it was. This implies for the engineer what is called a spectrum that is constant across all frequencies, which means in practice that such a process requires infinite power to run it. That's right: if you plugged your white noise machine into the wall socket you'd drain all energy that ever had been or would be created, and it would still not run. Which means you can't trot down to Best Buy and find one of these babies on the shelf. But it represents in some sense the most random behavior to be found in the universe. And it obeys laws.

The law it follows when its paths are summed (meaning integration, for those who have a smattering of education, be it formal or self) is Wiener's process, the fictive pure Brownian motion without physical impediments like drag. Of course, as noted previously Einstein broke the law with this creation since it had no bounds on its velocity. In fact, it turned out to be so irregular in its trajectories, if you can call them such, that it covers an arbitrarily large distance in any finite interval of time. And all the while with hands never leaving the body, so to speak — that is to say, always turning sharply while remaining continuous. So of course this perky speed demon refused to obey the speed limit of light. Note the adjective for the trajectories was continuous, not smooth. Because these paths are so jagged they have corners on the corners, you might say. For a mathematician this means the paths have no derivatives anywhere, which is to say that if you look at the process's path differences over disjoint intervals of time, they will be independent of one another. If you consider smaller and smaller such disjoint time intervals, you begin to see where white noise gets its bad behavior. You can observe this process for any amount of time you wish; the observation is useless because the process will start from the last observed spot as if it were born afresh in that moment.

And so you ask, How the hell can such a thing as this obey laws? Much like politicians and corporate executives (an interchangeable lot, actually) obey laws. Like when I wrote above that the integrated white noise trajectories are Wiener process sample paths; though formally true, that was a lie. There are a couple lies; one simple due to Wiener and one more complex due to Kyioshi Ito that was made intuitive by Steve Rosencrans in some course notes. Think smoothing out second-order wiggles, at least in the Rosencrans experience of Ito. Still pretty jagged, even at that, and giving rise to pesky second-order wiggles engineers ignore at their peril, especially when unaccounted for said second-order wiggles fuck up the extended Kalman filter's gain, causing it to crash and burn.

And now as we finally peak, take a gander down upon erose terrain and behold an endless landscape of bottomless crevices and twisted precipices. Terrifying. But in the aggregate tamed. Because if we have enough riders on these trails, we can average them and get deterministic. That's right. This nearly totally random monster (Gaussian, for those who care about such things) of Wiener's via Einstein provides us a solution to a deterministic problem. Bound some region nicely and give it some functional preconceptions meeting a smattering of conditions and then release a passel of these maniacal wrigglers, capturing them as they try to cross the perimeter and averaging them with respect to those conditioned preconceptions and you solve a classical deterministic partial differential equation.

How the hell does this happen? Well, let's skip the long story and just say that the friendly little BM (as the Brownian motion in its incarnation as Wiener process is often nicknamed) is related to an operator called the Laplacian that lives in infinite-dimensions. This operator has a long history in mathematics and physics. Moreover this operator can be related to the diffusion of heat, the heat equation which is supposed to model the flow of heat via a partial differential equation. Deterministically.

For example, take an infinite wire with perfect insulation and hit it with an outrageously hot torch at a single spot. Just for an instant. Then the heat distributes along this wire according to this heat equation. But there are some issues. For one, no matter how far away from the torch you hold this infinite wire, at torch touch you immediately feel some heat. That somehow seems wrong, but then no one has ever seen an infinitely long, perfectly insulated wire. What is curious is that the Brownian particle dances in the same manner as the heat distributes, which explains why it is compelled to get so far so fast.

Actually the dance of the BM is described probabilistically by the solution to this heat equation. That is to say, the heat equation lays down the law to this floppy, twitchy, and unpredictable process. So this relationship isn't so surprising. Moreover, by choosing more general "elliptic" operators than the Laplacian one can get seemingly more exotic dancers. These are called diffusion processes, and what is amusing is the existence of people who apply this to finance. They have been involved in some remarkable disasters with their techniques, notwithstanding the Nobel prize for economics to the inventors.

The unpredictability of the noise process is kind of misleading anyway. One can make predictions but only in terms of the long run. It's a lot like when a misguided meteorologist claims that because climate scientists cannot predict the short term behavior, they cannot predict the long term either. That is simply false, as work with stable devices such as atomic clocks or gyroscopes demonstrates. Short term forecasts are notoriously bad with noise, but long term trends are better predicted because of averaging. There is a statistical tool developed by engineers for this sort of behavior in such devices, called the Allan variance.

Anyway, it turns out that noise can be used to construct the deterministic, and the deterministic lays down the law to noise. That was what I meant with the idea of weeds and noise: for me, that pesky Brownian motion is not noise so much as just another side of the regular world. Besides solving deterministic problems (albeit inefficiently in a numerical sense), it can also explore both the geometry and the topology of certain mathematical creations residing in arbitrary dimensions.

But for an engineer with a GPS receiver, noise can be a damned weed. And though we have been stuck on white noise, we also encounter what is sometimes called colored or pink noise. This noise has relationships with itself over time. One of the more bizarre variants is the so-called 1/f noise, which is related to fractals it seems. Benoit Mandelbrot is the guy to see about this, and all we can say here is that this noise is very unlike white noise. While white noise has no relationship to its own behavior at any time in the past, 1/f noise has self-relationships that go to the infinite past, whatever that is. It never forgets where it has been, so to speak, whereas white noise immediately forgets. Yet perhaps all these colored noises are the progeny of white noise, but that is way outside the realm of where we ought to go.

Noise permeates everything because so far as I can tell, everything is noise. Unless of course there is the not-noise and not-deterministic. That would be the haphazard, as my old friend and teacher Roger Carlson liked to call it. The opposite of determinism is haphazard, not random. For example, haphazard would be if your neighbors became rhinoceroses; worse, if the E. coli in your gut become rhinoceroses. Small ones, say. Statistical mechanics has no place for such events to occur often, though there is a famous theorem of Poincare regarding events eventually recurring no matter how small their probability (that is, no matter how contrived they may have been originally), so long as positive and you can wait long enough. Sort of a mathematical version of Murphy's law. But we don't expect to see it on the macro scale outside Kafka or Ionesco or similar fantasists. Laws of averages hold sway, keeping Wiener's homogeneous chaos blues away. Hopefully.

NOTES:

[1]http://g1.globo.com/Noticias/Ciencia/0,,MUL457062-5603,00-BACTE-RIAS+TAMBEM+PODEM+TER+VARIAS+PERSONALIDADES+DIZEM+CIENTISTAS.html

[2]http://www.nytimes.com/2008/04/22/health/research/22coli.htmlex=1366516800&en=f0b164c6d8797aa0&ei=5088&partner=rssnyt&emc=rss

[3] Bogus-speak is language with the intent of sounding scientific or precise. A terrifying example that has invaded the language is the use of impact to replace the noun effect and verb affect (and perhaps sometimes the verb effect, but this is not clear). Some have argued that this hideous abomination is akin to a fecal impaction of language (mouth turds refusing to budge), much like the use of awesome as an adjective to describe some triviality you might find slightly special. Impacted prose, particularly in the verb case, might be the result of broadcast journalists not being literate enough to grasp the difference between affect and effect, and hence choosing to smear the meaning of a once precise verb as substitute. That this is incorrect can be seen with a bit of reflection: media journalists (and perhaps print journalists, too) are not sufficiently literate to realize there is a difference between affect and effect as verbs (and have been known to use the noun affect when effect was meant).

The real culprit seems to be economists, who in their need for certification as scientists appropriated language and mathematical technique to become a modern cargo cult, emptily parodying physics like ceremonial magic with none of the result. Of course, the excuse is that they cannot control experiments as can physicists, in a lab, though I seem to remember neither Newton nor Einstein were able to bring our planetary system into a lab (or even the Sun and one planet). The actual difference is that when physical theories provide incorrect predictions (and the ability to predict is the hallmark of a theory), physicists replace those theories. Hence the perihelion of

Mercury, and relativistic versus classical mechanics. When an economic "theory" makes a prediction, a rare event, and it is wrong, the economist blames reality, not his own ideas. Though these rare events are not easy to come by, consider the beautiful mathematics of Black-Scholes, based on the theory of random processes known as martingales and their integration via Kiyoshi Ito's formula, and the debacle of Long Term Capital Management. A failure of the "theory" of economic engineering. Not the first, nor the last, given the prevalence of derivatives in our financial web. And the culprit, as it turns out, was reality. Out of step with a mathematical model pawned off as an "economic theory."

At any rate, the testimony of Crocker and Petraeus before Congress provides an instructive example of the use of bogus-speech in its most common form. Words like trajectory are employed to give an aura of determinism, of control, as if things are going as expected along the path to which they have been steered. The terms sound precise, scientific, as if taken from automatic control theory, but here the "trajectory" is the conversion of the new Iraqi government into a satrap of the US, an outpost in which to base troops for the empire. Clearly this is not going quite as determined by the initial conditions, at least as seen from the Pentagon or the Bush White House.

Reality is that bogus-speak is an elaborate form of smoke-blowing. When you hear it in most contexts you can be certain someone is bullshitting you. In its most common form, as before Congress, it pits one or more actors against an appropriately august body divided into two or more sides engaged in a zero sum game for which the speakers are tokens, said speakers comporting with appropriate demeanor presenting appropriate language which no one really understands but designed to make everyone concerned delude themselves and wallow in the obvious lie, or else use the lie as an appropriate ass-cover and perhaps excuse for later mea culpas. It is also used to help other parties not part of the august body, such as citizen-consumers, be at ease with what everyone knows in their heart to be a fucking lie. That is, it is part and parcel of a mass self-delusion.

Jim Chaffee is a software program (a virtual being). His work is the output of an interactive writing program invented by Maurice Stoker. Unlike the newer stand-alone parameter-driven models (batch processing) of which it was an early, pre-beta prototype, this program requires a human sitting at a computer interacting with the outputs. In that sense it is like APL or MATLAB. In fact, like MATLAB it runs toolboxes to produce short stories, essays, novels, and such. Of course, it is not possible to do anything truly creative, like proving mathematical theorems, with the program.

Chaffee's "biography" includes service as a Navy Hospital Corpsman in support of Marines in Vietnam; studies in mathematics at University of Missouri at Kansas City and Tulane leading to completion of all the requirements for the PhD except the dissertation, which he bagged to escape academic death; research work in the early stages of the Global Positioning System, with a number of published papers; starting and running an ultra-high tech R&D company. And like most action figures, indulging in absurdly promiscous sexual psychodrama, fucking his way across four continents. Though not adverse to sex with lone females, or with two or three of them simultaneously, he always got the maximal adrenaline rush from group gropes, orgies and swing parties, and misses swinging and whoring in Brazil, particularly in the public swing clubs and boates of Sao Paulo. He invented swing golf, giving new meaning to the expression eighteen holes.

But that is dull shit. Stuff that is moribund by today's standards of superheroes with drug and sexual problems, cocksucking politicians from Idaho and infinite mouth-to-brain ratio talking heads on shit like CNBC. So to beef up the resume/biography/legend to meet today's over-the-top standards, Maurice is working with the program Jim Chaffee and the economist Doctor Boozer Allan Hamilton to produce an autobiographical novel akin to On the Road, entitled Studies in Mathematical Pornography: American Dream. Look for it to eventually appear. in the meantime, keep your foreskin clean. Remember, the biggest drawback of the jungle is an elephant's foreskin, which brings to mind some of the female visages from CNBC and Fox News.

Mickey Z.

Father's Day:
My Dad and the Mob

From the mountains outside Rome to an apartment complex north of Houston, Michael A. Zezima, Sr. has seen enough and lived enough for several lives. The problem is, he rarely, if ever, tells anyone about it.

This is a man who performed his undercover duties so well that a mobster once asked him to be godfather to his child, a man who rode shotgun on 747s and was prepared to take a bullet for Ronald Reagan (major disagreement there). A man who witnessed the Nazis occupying his town, saw battle in Korea, had his sunglasses smashed by Hubert Humphrey . . . a man who stepped on John Gotti's expensive shoes. He's turned down million dollar bribes and stared down the barrel of a gun that miraculously jammed. My Dad has dealt with rogue CIA agents, was cross-examined by F. Lee Bailey, bonded with Golda Meir, hunted for the Son of Sam, and saw Geraldine Ferraro in nothing but her nightgown.

We were poolside at The Woodlands, Texas where my parents have retired. I was reading one of my Dad's wiseguy books, "Gangbusters: The Destruction of America's Last Great Mafia Dynasty" by Ernest Volkman, when I decided to share with him the author's theory on the origin of the term "mafia." Here's sort of how it went: Volkman believes that the roots go back as far as the eleventh century, when the Saracens ruled Sicily. He cites the term "mafiusu," a word that translates roughly as "beautiful" or "excellent," and explains it relates to the word "mafia"-which meant "place of refuge" and was similar to an Arabic expression. When the Normans eventually conquered Sicily, Volkman explains, small landholders waged guerrilla warfare from caves (the aforementioned places of refuge) and came to be known as "mafioso." This brought a smile to my Dad's face.

"Well, that's one theory," he said, before revealing a far more dramatic source.

It seems that after the French conquest of Sicily (I think it was during the Napoleonic wars) the locals were not treated well. The occupiers, while carrying out the task of exporting Sicilian livestock back to France, abused the Sicilian populace, driving them to covert action. Organizing behind the slogan of "morte ai Francesi Italia anela" ("death to the French, Italy cries"), farmers began to kill French soldiers and stuff them into the barrels that were designated for the purloined livestock. When those barrels reached France and the contents discovered, it had the same effect of waking to find a horse's head in your bed. The abuse of the Sicilians came to an abrupt halt.

Now, if you go back and check out the first letter of each of the words in that Sicilian slogan, they spell out "mafia." I have no idea if it's true, but I definitely like my Dad's theory better.

Mickey Z. is probably the only person on the planet to have appeared in both a karate flick with Billy "Tae Bo" Blanks and a political book with Howard Zinn. He is the author of ten books, including the upcoming novella, *Darker Shade of Green*, from Raw Dog Screaming Press. He can be found on the Web at mickeyz.net.

Kane X. Faucher

The Other London

Naturally, comparisons are dismal, worthless drivel — exercises in pointless dot-joining given to grammar school students to occupy their time. Others, such as rabidly polemical politicos, rely on comparisons of the sloppiest variety as rhetorical sport which exacerbate the condition of argument bloat, fabricating entire straw populations their effete hatred can bash away on. This we know, yet there is also a capacity to leverage comparison for the humorous effect of juxtaposition as a heuristic device. The readers here are most likely too old for geography lessons about places so dreary and of little interest, and yet this is precisely what we are going to discuss. Or, at the very least, use a comparison as a peg upon which to espalier the stiff, soiled garments to speak of one item.

You see, you readers there, and me over here, are in an awkward predicament on par with two people coming to the same cocktail party in the same cut and colour of evening wear. We both share the same name: we both live in London. Well, not quite. You see, we retained many of your names and yet we do not resemble you in the slightest. From the standpoint of urban geography, this is disorienting. My London is the recondite facsimile of your London, yet occulted in the arcane practice of heavy-borrowing of names that do not coincide with the substance of the original. This is beyond the overweening colonialist habit of naming streets after titles like King and Queen that one finds in just about every Canadian city, for we have aped many of your street names, and even in one instance the borough of Lambeth (which was an autonomous village until 1992 when it was annexed by the city despite an attempt by the Reeve to dub it the Town of Westminster in 1988).

Your London I need not say much about, for it is the one you wrestle through every day in your commutes, playing bowls, or slugging pints — whatever it is that genuine article Londoners do to occupy their time. Your London is more than ten times the age of my London. It also has well over twenty times the number of souls and soulless, so my London would be pulverized if ever we decided to have a *cite-a-cite* brawl. My London is the diminutive, derivative London, and, worse, may qualify for the term used to describe such nostalgically named cities: a skeuomorph. Not only that, but we are poor urban epigones, our Thames but a choked rill, our Dundas Street a warren of commercial flaccidity, our Piccadilly a suburban squiggle on the map. We took all your street names, threw them in a bag, and emptied them out to form what is now our urban geography that bears no likeness to your own. It is the urban planning version of Scrabble and our city forebears were struggling to form words with no vowels across a continent-wide board.

The difference in exotic travel reportage between our respective Londons is worthy of remark. Your method is to extract the similarities between what lies abroad and what is familiar at home, thereby revealing the fundamental redundancy of locations (perhaps as well to signal why travel is unnecessary, serial repetition of high modernism triumphant). For us, we begin with the redundancy preinstalled and aim to dress it up as anything but, yet we are poor at applying the veneer. This adheres, as well, to the way we market our benighted and derivatively named city. If you came here to report on my London, you would be pressed to draw any sort of equivalence beyond a few recognizable names set in a perplexing context. The best, at least fictional, rendering of your London was performed by your Will Self who was able to shrink it to two-thirds its size and fill it full of brachiating chimps — perhaps a more apt description of my London after all.

When I tell people I live in London, there is usually the need to qualify further to avoid confusion. "No, not London with Big Ben, the tube, and roast beef dinner, but the *other* London, situated in south-western Ontario, Canada, the London with the noxious brewery, railroads running through high density traffic areas, and the world's worst taco stand." The nominal confusion can sometimes serve as a potential benefit, and so do not be surprised to find some of my Londoners leaving interpretation up to the listener by failing to qualify which London they mean, and so therefore exploiting your good reputation for personal gain. It is uncertain why the usual naming conventions of other colonial towns did not seem to factor in the settling of this London. A trip to the gazetteer yields up several more proper designations that avoid redundant naming such as *New* England, *New* York, *New* Berlin, and so forth. So, the question remains as to why we did not opt for *New* London? Were the founding fathers of our diminutive burg counting on the confusion to re-route business interests from your London to this mine? Was our indolence so manifest that we decided to piggyback your reputation to increase our own geographical cachet? Are the many Englanders who first settled here so homesick that they opted for paving over their own denial by trying to recreate all the comforts of home as if marooned on an alien planet? Beyond confusing tourists, perhaps one explanation will suffice: my London may in fact be the nightmare version of yours in a parallel universe traversed by Alice. Yes, we are the bad trip of your London. And, if some horrible catastrophe ever befalls your London, well, I suppose you may transfer here and at least have the comfort of your name as well as keeping most of your mailing information intact.

You may find it flattering that we dedicated the naming of our streets, parks, and other urban features after your own, but if you paid us a visit, you would most likely be embarrassed that we took your historical names in vain. If our aim was to replicate the feel and tone of your London, it was a consummate botch, a dervish rendition of your native and cherished home. In Platonic terms, we do not even come close to qualifying as a copy — instead, we are a whipped together simulacrum, our colonial Adams of this pared down, grim Eden given the task of naming things without exercising any imagination or innovation. The only way our Londons would ever resemble one another would be if you all succumbed to a collective amnesia, shed close to 7.5 million residents, wrecking-balled all your landmarks, and arbitrarily shuffled your *A-Z*.

The serial repetition stamped upon this Canadian geography is in name only. To complain that we are not your mirror image would be crass since the last thing we need is redundant architecture. In other cities I have lived in, one of the most endearing qualities was in discovering that it was a mash-up accident, that no one was actually from the city, and that we just happened to converge there for a time as though the city itself was one vast train station. This London, however, is largely populated by deep-rooted generations, lending it the North American equivalent of dynastic history. My London was founded by a chap named Simcoe whose lofty vision was that it would one day serve as the capital of the then fledgling Canada, and hence the move to name it after your London was more the product of a hope and a wish. This act of naming was rejected by a few who thought the place terribly inaccessible. But the name stuck, whether this was because of proactive agitation to retain the name or for lack of any interest to call it something else, we were officially stuck with the name in 1832. Our history, unlike yours, does not carry many of the dramatic highlights of being overrun by Romans, Saxons, Danes, Jutes, Angles, and Normans, but we have been annexed by corporations as the go-to site for call centres that sop up some of our unemployed to tele-pester residents into signing up for another credit card. We have also been overrun by waves of ignorant neo-conservatives, hordes of biblical zealots, pickup-truck fleets of rural-minded homophobes, and the imperial Wal-Mart. And, as if an attempt to earn the use of your name, we even had our own Great Fire, a few devastating floods, and even the added dash of historical colour that only a cholera outbreak can provide.

We do not have the Queen summering here in a makeshift Buckingham Palace. Instead, we have a steel rhino made by a now deceased artist. I am certain your Queen would be welcome to ride it if she wanted to. We do not have as many places of historical interest — in fact, I cannot really think of one. "Historical" is rather relative, it seems, for we are quick to nail heritage plaques on anything older than disco. I can already hear the rasping chorus of complaint from my local Londoners, that I am giving short shrift to the deeply fascinating historical episodes and personages that make up our city's unique narrative. Such people are very proud to be in my London, which I suppose is a frame of mind an outsider like myself cannot grasp, especially when the whole place feels unbearably in the thick humidity of the present, and no appeal to history herself will throw open a window to let the bad air out. In my dim and narrow view of what properly constitutes pride, I usually reserve the term for things that are done particularly well. The closest I can conceive would be the pride Dr Frankenstein felt in creating something near to life from conniving tissue scraps from the graveyard.

Like my previous example of two party-goers coming in the same outfit, it may seem only natural that one of us will have to renounce our name. Who will blink first? Your London with its two millennia precedent or our measly two centuries eking by on luck or oversight? We could revert to our pre-colonial name of Kotequogong, but that is a bit of a mouthful, not to mention a bit long to put on our tourism brochure.

My London is a very confused idea, the kind that occurs in the throes of extreme febrility. A trip to Londonkiosk.ca does its level best to make the pitch of just how wonderful my London is. To quote: "London is known for its charming streets, unique attractions and old world charm." Indeed, especially if you find streets in horrid disrepair charming, if by unique attraction the masses of mentally ill people for whom there are no beds in our psych facilities, and if by old world charm one means all the nastiest principles of the old world tossed on a boat and banished to the new world. Perhaps they are describing your London when they speak of old world charm, or entire boroughs in my London are kept hidden with an advanced cloaking device only the elect can see. The website goes on in its hand-clapping enthusiasm to describe my London's ideal location, situated between Toronto and Detroit. Well, lots of other places share the same affliction — and being upwind of one puts us at the mercy of being downwind of the other. There is also mention of clean streets (again, perhaps cloaked) that are tree-lined (our downtown, in the absence of trees, has erected neon-coloured substitutes made of metal), with first class parks (they are scrub pastures infested with mangy squirrels and irritable geese dropping their Poisson distribution of mushy green guano), and diverse shopping (our downtown core collapsed when everything moved to the "big box" outskirts) and nightlife (if your choice of nightlife is to get into fist fights with barely of age college boys or have barely of age college girls vomit on your shoes). There is, however, plenty to do if you wear a sweater vest, are heavily medicated, and employ the word "zany" to describe things you are otherwise uncomfortable with. What the online brochure does not mention are the many colourful drunks and addicts that station themselves in our downtown, but lacking in the type of romantic charm your London's version of such people seem to possess. The attempt at making the sly pitch is hobbled with a lack of much to say.

As this document continues to grasp at straws, it makes mention of my London's many arts and culture venues in a city largely bereft of either. It is not as though we are devoid of those noble-minded practitioners, but that there is a mediocrity transom — if it does not cater to the slack-jaw "tox" populi of hobbyist landscapes or belligerent monster machines pulverizing one another, then like most cultural offerings it may just languish in an arts listing at the back of a free entertainment zine. The heft of our artistic production advertised to the world would duly render us comfortably dumb. The glitz and flash of city council's proposed investment programs as detailed in its own new glossy brochure is self-confident that we will be fooled by the overt rhetoric of ambiguity that sides with vacuity and well-meaning signifiers that mask a chronic, flagrant lack of concern for my London's cultural producers and the few remaining programs that administer the paltry scraps thrown its way.

The new brochure, which details my London's strategic plan up until the unimaginably distant year of 2026, is seemingly a well-intentioned document designed to allay any misgivings the residents of this city may have with the way public tax revenues are bungled to fund pet projects. My London should be world-famous for its "strategic plans" and "visions", and local government can be seen bruiting these about, prancing around like heroic grandees selling us on the brighter tomorrows that always seem to lapse when that future date comes and it is time to push the best-by date another decade.

My London does have a pool of vibrant, committed, and intrepid world-class artists in every field, but they ignobly suffer a lack of support and recognition. Instead, my London is packaged as a great place for curling. No mention in the tourism brochures of a very active contingent of artist-run centres, and absolutely devoid of any promotion of London's real grassroots: the artists themselves. Is this the city that culture forgot? Not at all. We have a formidable stable of marketable musicians, writers, dramaturges, actors, and visual artists, and yet what support do they get? There may be a prevailing assumption that any artist who says s/he comes from London may as well have just crawled out of a swamp.

Back to our tourism accolades. What I find particularly telling is this: "if you are here during the summer months your visit would not be complete without an authentic Double Decker London (England)-style Bus Tour departing daily from London City Hall." I can now understand why the rest of our bus system is so poorly funded. The selling of authenticity, so blatantly advertised, does imply that the remainder of the city is the opposite. There's nothing like being jostled about on an authentic bus to enjoy inauthentic sightseeing. And if you are here in the winter, you can come ski on our Boler Mountain, yet another example of our tendency to exaggerate given that it is more of a bee sting — I live right by it and I hardly need a sherpa to reach the summit of this "bunny slope of the Himalayas."

However, my London is very proud of its nickname, that being the "Forest City" because, at some point long ago, we had countless acres of forest, just like everywhere else. The tourism guide tells us that at one point my London was an isolated destination that one could only access by hacking through the forest. And I suppose the same thing can be said of many leper colonies. A recent study undertook to count them all — 4.4 million or about 12 per person. Since every October we are assailed by a plague of predator-less Asian ladybugs, perhaps these tree-counters could be reassigned to populate another factoid to tell us just how many of the pests we are entitled to per person.

Another particularly risible laudatory self-praise would be this: "London is a thriving city, evident of its skyscrapers in its skyline" (as opposed to its waterline?). Here I believe they must have confused my London for your London. Our skyline is not exactly Chicago's. Subsequent to boasting about our tree-choked, charming-streeted, megalith-skyscraped, Himalayan-mountained, roaring-rivered, haute-cultured metropolis, the rather thin tourist spiel announces our economic prowess with "insurance" being in the top three. I would recommend a revision of that previously quoted line to read: "London is an expiring city, evident in its tottering derelict buildings in its crumbling skyline as testament to its moribund course." My London is not only between Toronto and Detroit, but between the Scylla of small-town corruption and the Charybdis of urban entropy.

My London has one peculiar charm, and I mean charm in the witchcraft sense, perhaps best expressed as a hex proper. It has a propensity for luring optimists. These optimists, exiles and cast-offs from their own native cities, come here and are immediately disgusted with the place. But that is not all. They do not slump in on themselves, sagging with resignation like so many other new residents. No, they thunder about what needs to be done, how they will scoop out the crusted bits of tumbledown east end, script brilliant mass transit plans, or mend all our open downtown sores with their construction money. The developers who come all starry-eyed and drunk on their own soft-furred cinematic visions are the ones who fare the worst when they cannot reverse our rack and ruin cityscape. The clouds they glide in on are the ones they find themselves hobbling under, on their way to make their fortunes in places more amenable to refurbishing. The vastness of their ideals never seem to thrive under these spirit-killing conditions; progressive urban planners present grand makeovers to make the city a city which are scuppered at the paper stage by chronic underfunding, and bistros with chic urban appeal go largely without patrons until the prohibitive municipal taxes finally drive them away. It will take more than just the application of a bit of rouge and an eyebrow pluck to doll up a city in dire need of a face-lift.

The displacement of my London from any reliable context has found it snuggled into its sandy basin as I judder along in a bus, looking out at an accidental city that squeezed itself, an afterbirth idea, from an identity crisis into the resigned neglect of its own potential. While I am waiting to make a connection, the newly planted electronic board with bus arrival/departure times digitally mock us all for impossible waits as we shiver or boil depending on season. White hip-hop boys trafficking openly in drugs swagger with a gait they identify with black culture in a space sadly devoid of it, but look more to me like the affliction of incipient polio or some other neuromuscular disorder. They project hoots from across the street to one another, or else vomit or toss a few punches. The chronic reflux of bad social fashion elbows for supremacy along with bad manners. One young man with a hot air balloon for a coat stencilled with commercial gangland script, plays the part of a Carolingian as re-imagined by Spike Lee. Standard orange-hide work boots are re-assigned their function as fashion, tongues lolling out and laces trailing behind in a skein. He collides into me and is ready with a combative face contorted with disdain, but sees I am no prey to his feeble masculinity lost in his puffy jacket and so leaves me to my own entitled and personal piece of territory. The scurry of their kind alloying with the fast and slow beads of regular commuters and idling downtownies is played out beneath the exquisitely carved fronts now occupied by pawn shops, discount cell phone services, hobby shops, and soft-porn boutiques. Facades from the 1920s are rimed with craftsmanship, windows tall and brazen, testament to an earlier era of largesse, splendour, and pride now dried jerky chewed off by the steady wave of dereliction and neglect. Each wedge of regally-carved optimistic architecture hard against one another, a historical masonic weight settled on the back of the deracinated business descendants. If one were to take a time-lapse video from my downtown London's salad days to the present it would be to see a string of bright lights shorting out in sequence, only to have their bankrupted business bulbs replaced to give off a fainter, sallower light.

Just up Dundas, beyond the clock tower stubbornly keeping time at the crossing at Richmond, gestures at upscale taste gleam from a diminutive condo with a pricey bistro tucked beside it, the only declaration of posh against a phalanx of gritty bargain shops. The abrupt John Labatt Centre, named after the nearby brewery that saddles the wind with its yeasty belches, houses popular acts and monster truck rallies across from the stump phallus of the courthouse built in the blocky minimalist style of the 1960s. Dundas describes a clinamen, the beginning of which is the glassy Museum London, an art gallery re-christened to bank on the chic naming practices of MOMA, resulting in confused tourists dropping into the London Arts office asking where the London art gallery is. Dundas then swerves into what is called The Forks where one of its tines is little more than a slender cul-de-sac while the other runs over a choppy iron bridge. A pitchfork, really, or a fork of pitch surface. The fork is suggestive not of the roadway, but the Thames River, two brown slashes between steep banks that resolve into a low-lying park that is submerged every spring thaw. A new and expensive fountain raised on a berm spews the Thames back into itself, a loop completing an unintended analogy of the city itself, fretting with its own short, dull, recursive history.

The Thames River, hardly coextensive with your own, seems to hold enduring fascination among our local poets who versify about its history, meaning, and attempt to flex the atrophied muscles of their metaphors to speak of its direction, life-sustaining force, and all else that pertains to a vermiculating sluice of water that never asked for or warranted poeticizing. Of course, I find all river poetry to be monotonous, as I do any geographically based poetry — but it keeps our poets flush with material, a wet subject for dry wordplay. Beyond being a confining scratch-board for poets, it is also a conduit for garbage. Gnarled aggregates form ferries that pluckily make landfall, ragged Styrofoam plinths accreted with miscellany are tangled up in the cattails with miniature dinghy pop cans and diminutive U-boat beer bottles. Algae twists in with the wreathing of plastic bags taking on the appearance of Halloween stretch-cotton cobwebbing. Dipping any exposed skin into the river leaves a glossy sheen that takes much scrubbing with dish soap to remove, most likely due to the farm and industrial waste fed into this slurry upriver.

London's commitment to nature's splendour recurs every few years with a fierce debate on whether or not there ought to be a deer cull in the western edges of the city. Residents of the Oakridge suburb kvetch that the deer are greedily munching their hostas and annuals and so due recompense for housing sprawl co-opting deer ranging territory is to have them shot. Never mind that a company was willing to give free samples of contraceptives to curb the deer population since that solution was not suitably barbaric to appease the sanguine needs of a people who only want nature on their own terms — preferably behind impassable fences or locked up in cages at the zoo. Bambi finds few friends in London, and the Malthusian cull results in a significant drop in the price of venison.

My London is also split into the usual orientating quadrants of north, east, west, south. These are subdivided into old north and old south, but the east and west are left intact as a spanning ellipsis, hopelessly adrift on either side. Old north contains many of the yellow- and honey-brick homes, the closest of which to the downtown core have been converted into lawyers' offices and chiro-quack clinics. Old north seems to include the pomp of the University of Western Ontario with its impressive stone edifices looming over or beside more modern additions. Old South, what was the last stop of London's discontinued trolley service, is one of those communities that contain within it the gentrified enclosure of the Wortley Village, an eye-pleasing neighbourhood buffered from the swarthiness of downtown by the loop of the Thames River and a thick sentinel wall of trees. The east with its slate-sided facades, has long since been a ghettofication experiment, a social pretzel of the undesirable, drug-addled, and miserable. Adelaide Street, also known as the backbone between good and evil, is a stark border running north-south between the more opulent homes of Old North and the crumbling despoilment of a once more prosperous neighbourhood. Banting House, the modest home where Dr Frederick Banting briefly occupied before discovering insulin, has done little to repair the pancreatic slab of the fleshy east end. My first apartment was a loft in a converted bubble gum card factory right beside the Banting House Museum, and my first memory of my London was having a beer at the sign-busted St. Regis Tavern, among old drunks with unchecked diabetes, one of them falling off the picnic table and declaring loudly, "I broke my ass!" So, I thought to myself, this is London. What I did not know then, but would later discover in my long romps through the city's intestinal tract on many a beery, idling graduate student night, was that this was an emblematic moment of what could be expected in the average night in my London.

London West feels tacked on, a pre-fab suburban flatland metastasizing around enormous box store plazas. It is less a romantic frontier carved out of the wildnerness as a peaceful hinterland savagely beaten back and bulldozed to make way for the rolling out of identical two-car garages and woodchip landscaping. The area named Whitehills with its Blackacres Boulevard sits in Manichaean relation to Whiteacres Boulevard where Whitehills and its pastel-hued homes end. On Sarnia Road, between Whitehills and Hyde Park, there is a rickety one-lane bridge owned by the CN railroad where traffic has to alternate three vehicles at a time between two growing slabs of neighbourhood. Further west, there is Byron, where I am situated. Byron — uncertain if named after the club-footed aesthete — was, like everything surrounding London, the municipal writ of annexing whatever London's own expansion would find itself butting against. Nowhere near as leaping as Toronto and its GTA that gobbles rather than nibbles, it is only a matter of time until the nearby towns like Lambeth (too late) and Ilderton lose their autonomy, just as it is only a matter of decades until the big fish of Toronto eats this little predatory fish of London. The process is to turn these towns into de facto suburban fringes of the city, expanding its rim until hopefully my London will touch two Great Lakes to the north and south. This indelicate dental surgery writ geographically takes the pointillist map of this parenthetical piece of Ontario and attempts to extract the impacted teeth to give the region a better smile. If only it were so simple and forthcoming a procedure, but there is no vision or method beyond what the greedy developers see as prime land to pump and dump their vast carpets of shoddily built homes to house families who can huddle closer to their Wal-Martian drips.

As a side note, and now as a landed Byronite in what is left of the picturesque environs, Byron changed names a few times in its history from Westminster to Hall's Mill to what it is known as today: a tuck-away of London. It boasts the country's sixteenth largest gravel pit for those gravel pit connoisseurs among you who are planning to tour this country's top 20 gravel pits. Between Boler Mountain (or "bump") and the pit, Byron is most likely blessed with having the highest and lowest topographical features. It is also home to London's most obscene and exotic insects, including what my wife and step-children refer to as "the Byron Bug" — a nasty looking weevil with sloth-like motion (note: the only entomological reference I can find on Google refers to a 1961 study by W.W. Judd so I cannot confirm the accuracy of my family's preferred nomenclature for this feather-footed friend). Amazonian moths, caterpillars, and the like are also creepy-crawly habitues. The regular swarms of ants, flies, spiders, wasps, and beetles are trebled in Byron in an Old Testament way. The occasional fox or coyote ranges the backwoods, prompting us to take our three cats inside.

Politically, my London and the word "progressive" would

largely qualify as the kind of brazen free interpretation performed by first year undergraduates seeking to redefine basic words behind novelty encounters in the realm of deconstruction. This was one of the three-city stops on the US arch-conservative pundit Ann Coulter who is said to have told a Muslim student at the university to "take a camel" after babbling some nonsense on preventing Muslims on flights. The piri-piri polemical arete was met, in my opinion, with a bit of meek anger, and Coulter ought to have been hissed, badgered, and otherwise driven clean from my London — if not prohibited from appearing, no matter what the freedom of expression groups say. But hate speech is free speech in my London, a slurry of expressions and opinions held by those who mix Jesus and neo-conservative notions into a venomous excuse to hold "family values" festivals that screech against abortion yet have no moral problem with sending armies to shoot non-Christians.

But this is my decided binocular reportage — with one tourist's eye, and the other belonging to a resident who never felt he graduated from being a tourist. This despite my initial reason for coming here, which slowly coupled with reasons for staying. The lure of money that brought me here for the doctorate, meeting my future wife, and then marrying here — all of these benchmarks that were to function as tied directly to this city does not seem to suggest any association for me. These rites of passage performed in a vacuous location, a cloud of events passing through an arbitrary section of sky.

My London's landmarks emerge as personal anecdotes in an otherwise brashly thrown up set. I recall my visit by my friend and writer Anthony Metivier and his discovery of the "exclamation period" — a granite dedication to lost labour lives looking exactly the way he titled it, and the chapbook he loosely based it on. There was — not is — The Wick, a nickname for the old Brunswick Hotel across from the Greyhound station. It was — again, not is — a dingy punk bar with a freer interpretation of provincial liquor laws, its upper floors technically condemned and so a suitable place for traveling punk bands to practice and do drugs. And, even if the pique of intoxication or punk theology induced them to anarchize the hostelry, there was no way of busting up something already so busted. I recall in the fondness of furred drunken nights whiling away on their picnic tables, a back patio ringed by a fence where a head or two would pop up to conduct a little underground commercial transaction. In view of the bus station, an Arabic corner store, and a rising condo tower edging out what sparse sunlight hit the patio, it was one of the few drinking holes — perhaps literally — that had any character at all. The new owner was eager to demolish it to transform the space into the more level profit of another pay-lot, but the carcinogenic insulation would have entailed a costly extraction by Haz-Mat suited specialists, and so a "mysterious arson" dispensed with any such expenditure. It should be stated that every legitimate effort to protect the squat edifice with heritage status was denied by most of city council, and that I've not heard of any investigation into the arson. To the cynical eye, it was an expedient means of banishing an undesirable cultural element, or else dispersing this diaspora to become diluted among the other drinking establishments.

I did not choose my London, nor did it choose me. When I was younger and more environmentally-dependent than I am now (or, I should say, I used my complaints against where I lived as an excuse for not being "inspired" to work), I would have rejected London as a suitable place to write in. Six years have passed, and I am still here, and I've discovered that it doesn't really matter where I am: the writing will ebb and flow according to its own internal logic. I find this very interesting since this is a city with not much to draw people to it, let alone linger for as long as some of us have. Some will call it an oasis between the highway escape chute between Toronto and Windsor, but an oasis of what still remains to be convincingly qualified.

If only my London could have poached more than your name. This is no encomium to your London whatsoever, but our frumpy bush league problems are chronic and absurd. For the tenth largest city in Canada, one might be tempted to believe that we would have fixed a lot of our problems, but instead we have invented new ones. For starters, the rolling epidemiological experiment of our bus system is a mass transit blight. A vital plank in My London City Hall's eight-point strategic initiative, the bus system — my preferred or no-choice-but mode of getting about — is still poorly managed. Despite our local leaders' claims to its importance as an environmentally sound alternative, and the surging price of gas, I am curious as to why the bus system continues to go so grievously underfunded. In terms of showing true leadership to honour brave new words, I would like to see the mayor and all the councillors take the bus for one solid week to witness for themselves what average, bus-commuting Londoners contend with on a daily basis. Perhaps this would retire the seeming "let them eat cake" attitude when they deliberate on public transportation funding in the next city budget.

The other bone of contention would be our garbage collection which seems measured according to the Mayan calendar. In my view, a week is seven days, not eight with countless exceptions divided by the square root of pi plus or minus the current municipal tax rate. I shouldn't have to take out my sextant and astrological charts to know when it is legal to put out my blue box of empty whiskey bottles. Admittedly, this is a trifling complaint, and nowhere near as serious as the railways that still cut across our major roadways, chugging slowly through during rush hour.

But that is quite enough of my little fang job, this rotten assessment about the city where I live. I can tell you that despite all its objectionable nonsense I don't find it so awful that I would consider fleeing. However, nor would I be the one to tap to give your Londoners any tourism advice if it would mean that you would actually spend valuable holiday time in my London. If you do, despite my aforementioned "highlights" of what you can expect as a recipe of dissuasion, I would recommend our authentically displaced "Monarch of the Road" so that you may delight in our botched mimicry and nominally-based homage. Regardless of our mash-up of your London, I can more foresee that you will experience an acute claustrophobia at every mention of your London area's names set in alien contexts, as though your boroughs were inescapably stretched and distorted across the Atlantic, your London rebuilt in a southwestern Ontario gully by a gang of confused adulators throwing up a mythical revision in a carnival fun mirror.

Kane X. Faucher is a cheeky author of ten or so books and a multitude of articles, poems, essays, reviews, short fiction, and miscellanea that nomadically traverse with ease from high falutin irrealism, impregnable polemical fiction, post-VisPo, vulgar gonzo, complex theory, journalistic reportage, contemporary art catalogue essays, political tracts, and crotchety Pound-style criticism. A chameleon of a scribe, an incorrigible maverick, and perhaps even a Wildean dilettante, he was won a smattering of modest awards in both literature and academia. He has been called many things, not all of them nice.

Kevin Sweeney

from **Drac the Ripper:**
Was Bram Stoker the Whitechapel Murderer?

The Writing Of *Dracula*

. . . stories and legends about witches, werewolves and vampires . . . may have been a way of explaining outrages so hideous that no one in the small and close-knit towns of Europe and early America could comprehend such perversities . . .
— Douglas, John and Mark Olshaker, *The Cases that Haunt Us*, 2001

So then, what facts can be assembled to give credence to our argument that Bram Stoker not only committed the murders, but fictionalised them into the legendary novel *Dracula*?

Well, the first and most crucial piece of evidence is the fact that he confessed as much. From Stoker's Preface to Icelandic edition of *Dracula*, 1901; "The strange and eerie tragedy which is portrayed here is completely true, as far as all external circumstances are concerned . . . Many people remember the strange series of crimes that comes into the story a little later — crimes which, at the time, appeared to be supernatural and seemed to originate from the same source and cause as much revulsion as the infamous murders of Jack the Ripper!"

So, having admitted that he was writing about those crimes we take the next logical step of assuming that he must have been the perpetrator.

Dracula is one of those rare works which has become a part of modern world myth; it is a story that everyone knows, even if they have never read the book . . . or at least, the general thrust of the story is well understood. Though it was by no means the first literary working of the vampire story (precedents include Sheridan Le Fanu's *Carmilla*, or even such Penny Dreadful titles as *Varney The Vampire, or, The Feast of Blood!*) it is by far the most well known. It is believed that Dracula himself has been portrayed on the big screen only slightly less often then Sherlock Holmes, in a bewildering varied spectrum of work covering nearly every year since films were first made, from faithful adaptations of Stoker's book through to the bizarre blaxploitation sub-genre classic *Blacula*. The figure of the Count has even become so established that he has passed into the realm of archetype; no longer a figure of fear, he adorns boxes of a popular American breakfast cereal.

Well known indeed . . . but as with so many things which have become so familiar, the majority of people really know nothing about Dracula, the book or the character.

A brief summary of the story; a wealthy East European aristocrat arranges to move from his isolated castle to the bustling metropolis of London. His every step along the way is filled with bizarre occurrences and bad deaths, until gradually it becomes apparent to a small group of people that the man is in fact a monster, stepped whole out of myth, a member of the undead who must feed on the blood of the living. He has supernatural abilities and seems unstoppable, and yet the group decide to try, because this creature threatens the whole of humanity with his presence . . . because whomever he feeds from becomes like him. What ultimately motivates Dracula is his desire to; "go through the crowded streets of your mighty London, to be in the midst of the whirl and rush of humanity, to share its life, its change, its death, and all that makes it what it is . . . " where, as Harker later realises; " . . . for centuries to come he might, amongst its teeming millions, satiate his lust for blood . . . "

The story is told in the form of journal entries, phonograph recordings, newspaper clippings and so, a method which builds up a fragmented picture from many viewpoints.

This is in its barest form the story. But, underneath the fear and horror of a "one man invasion" is a very different tale. Simply (crudely) put, *Dracula* is about sex. More, it is about the complex emotions that come with sex, and the clash of genders. We shall deal with this presently.

The Whitechapel murders case was officially closed in 1896 . . . the year before "Dracula" was published. Now, if the book was published in 1897, it would be reasonable to believe that it was written in 1896. Stoker is reported to have spent eight years researching the work, which would put the start of this research in the year of the murders, 1888.

The novel opens less than a month after the death of Emma Smith and concludes three days before the date on which the Ripper claimed his last-known victim.

But what could have inspired the idea for wrapping the crimes in the myth of the vampire? Possibly the newspapers of the day themselves, who were often found using the term;

" . . . vampires, of whom society has the right to be quickly rid, without too much attention to the theories of mental experts." From *The Daily Telegraph*, 10 September, 1888.

"[The Whitechapel murderer] puts all the vampire stories of fiction to bed and tucks them up for the rest of their natural lives . . . " From *The Sunday Referee*, 16 September, 1888.

"It is so impossible to account, on any ordinary hypothesis, for these revolting acts of blood, that the mind turns as it were instinctively to some theory of occult force, and the myths of the Dark Ages arise before the imagination. Ghouls, vampires, bloodsuckers . . . what can be more appalling than the thought that there is a being in human shape stealthily moving about a great city, burning with the thirst for human blood?" From *East London Advertiser*, 6 October, 1888.

Here was a book practically begging to be written; all it needed, perhaps, was a little inside knowledge. Consider the connections; the vampire bites the throat and drinks the blood, whilst the Ripper slit the throats. To kill a vampire the head must be completely severed; in the worst of the Whitechapel murders the throats were cut so deeply that the vertebrae were nicked, almost cutting the head free of the body. These are obvious parallels.

Do we need to mention cannibalism? The vampire who drinks blood, the Ripper who eviscerated his victims and ate parts?

How many dead women are "turned", that is to say, receive "special attention", in *Dracula*? Five we know of, the three Brides, Lucy, and Mina (who is only partly turned; though the burial service is read over her, effectively making her "dead".) This corresponds to the canonical five victims of the Ripper. Interesting that three of these victims had names and aliases that were remarkably similar (Mary Ann Nichols, Catherine Eddowes AKA "Mary Anne Kelly", and Mary Jane Kelly"); perhaps we see no difference between these three with their close names, and the ill defined trio of Brides?

But then we ask the question; why would Stoker confess?

The simplest answer seems to be because of what Poe described as "the Imp of the Perverse", the need for a criminal to confess, to crow. The novel is one long boast.

Dracula's character is boastful, and oddly praised by other characters. Jonathon Harker writes; " . . . he would have made a wonderful solicitor, for there was nothing that he did not think of or foresee . . . " And further; " . . . learning beyond compare, and a heart that knew no fear and no remorse."

Not to mention the way the Count is continually seen as attractive by every female in the book; praise of this sort is surprisingly common. This kind of behaviour is common in psychopaths (here written directly into the mouths of the characters) crowing over their achievements and generally regarding themselves as being above the mass of men.

So finally, what reason have we to suppose that, these murders committed, the killing ended? This we leave the last word to Eric Ambler's 1963 book, *The Ability to Kill*, in which a halt to such activities could be because " . . . having achieved an apotheosis of horror, he had at last exorcised the evil that haunted him."

The nature of this horror will be explored later . . . .

Stoker's Fingerprints

Having erected our house of cards, now it seems as though actual evidence is needed to support our case. First, we require motivation, and secondly, we need means. Along the way we shall sprinkle in a few interesting facts that do nothing to directly support the theory, but when taken cumulatively and not examined in too much detail will help convince the dullard in each of us that yes, something fishy is going on (regardless of whether it is or not.)

Motivation. Stoker wrote an article for the *Daily Chronicle* in 1908 on the subject of censorship, an attack on "works of shameful lubricity" that were "corrupting the nation". He states that "It is as natural for man to sin as to live" and that it is therefore necessary to contain this "force of evil" (those "works") to stop them exploiting "the forces of inherent evil in man."

Then, oddly, he adds "The word man here stands for woman as well as man; indeed, women are the worst offenders in this form of breach of moral law."

The nail in the coffin?

"A close analysis will show that the only emotions which in the long run harm are those arising from the sex impulses, and when we have realised this we have put a finger on the actual point of danger."

Interesting use of language throughout, with the constant repetition of the word "evil" coupled with terms such as "harm" and "danger", and the explicit fingering of women as the main culprits.

We recall these words from earlier; "I was a very strong man. It is true that I had known weakness. In my babyhood I used, I understand, to be often at the point of death. Certainly till I was about seven years old I never knew what it was to stand upright. I was naturally thoughtful and the leisure of long illness gave opportunity for many thoughts which were fruitful according to their kind in later years."

What thoughts? And to what kind? At such an early age of development are the first foundations for later behaviour made; we think of Renfield, confined by his own illness, his mental illness, and the sadistic pleasures he takes in tormenting weaker creatures, a sure sign of a psychopath. More personal reminiscences drawn from memory on Stoker's part?

Then we recall that Stoker's own mother was a feminist. The young Stoker, bed bound, would have been attended to every day by a strong willed woman, his early mind shaped by these impressions; another classic warning sign of possibly later psychopathic tendencies, "the oppressive mother" is almost as strongly indicated as a contributing factor as the torment of lesser creatures. Could a later hatred (in public, his attack of women as the fount of social ills) of the feminine sex be tied up with his upbringing?

Whilst you consider that, consider this; according to the novel, Dracula keeps six of his coffins at 197, Chicksand Street, Mile End New Town. Chicksand becomes Osborn Place which crosses Brick Lane to continue as the ill-famed Flower and Dean Street where three of victims had lived. This address is at the epicentre of where the murders took place in East London.

There is a reoccurrence of the idea of "the East" all through *Dracula.* The Count comes from Transylvania and lands at Whitby, then takes residence in Carfax. All Eastern points. The murders took place in the East end of London. Two plus two equals five.

A lot of foreigners were accused of being the Ripper (Severin Antonovich Kłosowski; Aaron Kosminski; Michael Ostrog; John Pizer . . . all Eastern Europeans) and aristocracy as well (Royal conspiracy theory); Dracula, an aristocratic foreigner, settling in the East End, a very different place to the West end Stoker inhabited. A dichotomy here as clearly marked as the difference between the everyday "business" side of a psychopath, and the darker passions. This dual nature was very much in the public mind of the time, as we shall see when we turn to another classic horror story of that age, and how it ties in with our theory, *The Strange Case of Dr. Jekyl & Mr. Hyde.*

Means. A belief that Jack was able to hide in plain respectable sight, like Hyde, lead some to believe that he was a master of disguise, which would mask his physical appearance, but also control his bloodlust somewhat; the Count has a smooth veneer, but is a monster under that nobility.

The Lyceum Theatre's production of *The Strange Story of Dr*

Jekyll & Mr Hyde was forced to close because of people who had seen the play began to mutter, suggesting that the star, Richard Mansfield, may have been leaving the stage "in character" at curtain close each night to head for Whitechapel . . . In 1888, the Lyceum had been managed by Bram Stoker for ten years. We remember that the victim Mary Kelly claimed to Lizzie Albrook to have a "relative" in the London theatre; a euphemism for "customer"?

Stoker ran the Lyceum Theatre; the Ripper was believed to be a master of disguise. Costume changes?

We read; "There are certain 'sexual perverts' to whom the myth of Dr. Jekyll and Mr Hyde is perfectly applicable. They hope, at first, to be able to gratify their 'vices' without compromising their public characters. If they are imaginative enough to see themselves, little by little, in a dizziness of pride and shame, they give themselves away . . . " from Simone de Beauvoir's classic essay, "Must We Burn Sade?"

This "dizziness of pride and shame" which gives them away is the Imp of the Perverse mentioned before; and which, by writing *Dracula* as a fictional confession, Stoker was able to circumvent compromising his public persona. Duh.

As already noted, he moved in the same social circles as Prince Albert Christian Victor, Walter Richard Sickert (who toured with Irving's Lyceum Theatre Company) and Lord Randolph Churchill. Add to these men, each identified as suspects, the possibility that Lewis Carroll could well have visited the theatre during Stoker's time there, and the fact that Francis Tumblety, a man who Chief Inspector John Littlefield believed a good candidate for the Ripper, was a friend of Hall Caine, the author to whom *Dracula* is dedicated, and you have a good deal of evidence which is not even circumstantial.

None of this linking him to other suspects does anything to really strengthen the argument, and neither does Stoker corresponding with one of the detectives who investigated the murders, though perhaps this informed Mina Harker's employing criminology methods to track Dracula, citing the well known expert of the time Cesare Lombroso.

Using early forms of profiling, nowadays the favoured tool of those who hunt serial killers, to pursue a supernatural creature?

Odd, no?

No.

The truth is if there were enough evidence to positively identify the murderer, let alone the kind of mind bogglingly distorted reasoning displayed here as a caricature of other such works, then there would be no industry for the endless books of speculation.

CONCLUSION

Anyone having read this far with at least one eye open and two brain cells to rub together will have deduced by careful examination of the text that we do not actually consider Bram Stoker to be a serious contender for being Jack the Ripper; we hope, in fact, that we have not been overly heavy handed in ramming home the fact that the vast majority of so-called "Riperology" is ham fisted clutching for blood money, staining names and reputations in a wild free fall of laugh-out-loud "logic" and contrived "evidence."

The reader may wonder that few references are given throughout the text; we crave an indulgence, as this is the last trick of those who build skyscrapers of cards, to extensively reference the known facts of the case and thus disguise their wild suppositions between walls of impressive looking text composed of page numbers, publishing houses, and dates. As we do not desire to trick anybody (the ridiculous title of this satirical monograph is the first clue of this intention) we choose to confirm that everything written as "fact" is just that, and have clearly indicated in the text by means of farce and sarcasm what is mere wind.

Kevin Sweeney, noun. Lives in C/Ford, prefers Bangkok. Working on a series of metafictional texts collectively called The Stratagem, ranging from the *Sideshow P.I.* series (with Nathaniel Lambert) to *Exeunt Alice* (with Lewis Carroll.) *Drac the Ripper* was originally published under the heteronym Patrick Joseph, a long term member of the GIB whose scribblings owe as much to Momus as to Eris.

Adam lowe

Digitise This

Language is changing. Literature is also changing. It's about time we threw aside slavish devotion to tradition and embraced the changes that can work for us as writers and readers. It's time literature became cross-fucked!

When putting together my novella, *Troglodyte Rose,* I used a number of different techniques: forcing them into crazed copulation to breed monstrous hybrid creatures. Originally the project was going to be an 'illustronovella', which is the mongrel bastard of sequential art (as in comics) and straightforward prose. This reinvigorated the writing process, adding a certain electric jouissance. Flitting between prose and script became an erotic encounter, with two bodies entwining and spawning new meanings. Like a tub of Vaseline, it made writing greasier and stickier, but also enhanced my pleasures. I was liberated of the courtship we novel-writers have with vigorous technical detail. When I was writing the script for the sequential art, I didn't have to think about sentence structures, metaphors, and showing and not telling. Instead I just described, in voyeuristic detail, how I fantasised the images would look. It was like writing pornography: fast, exhilarating, and for someone who's never done it before, sordid in the way Hunter S. Thompson is when you've only ever read Jane Austen.

My prose sections were jizzed out in almost poetic slivers, gluing the action-packed segments of script into bareback loveliness. As Douglas Thompson later said of the book:

> I have long harboured the hope that film might have changed writing in much the same way as photography changed painting, and that we are therefore in a bold new era where novels don't rely on the sequential any longer, but are a series of paragraphs each as good as a poem.

The writing was coarse yet sexy, light yet thoughtful, meaningful and purely physical, like the best sex always is. Consider the literary arousal had by stroking the following:

> We are inside Hell. How can I describe it any other way? I can feel the fires of the glassworks. I can smell the sulphurous breath of our chthonic gods. I live in squalid darkness and breathe filthy air. My name is Rose and I've never seen the sky.

To keep the experience more passionate, more vigorous, I alternated between slow and gentle, hard and fast, deep and close, teasing and rammed down the throat. I interspersed slower, more introspective prose sections with fast-paced, rampaging script for art sequences. Unfortunately due to the artists' commitment to providing a serial for Tor.com, the overall project had to evolve, and the bastard hybrid required serious cybernetic reconfiguration, in the Donna Haraway sense.

In the end I opted to rape the Japanese light novel for the basis of the book's style and aesthetic. Those scripted sections I'd written, which were all about action and dialogue by necessity, were sluttily converted to prose that captured the same gasping pace and shuddering, orgasmic energy sequential art would have. Consider:

PAGE 1.

1 Underground. Outside a pharmaceutical store called Sindar's Pharmacy. Light comes from mirrors fixed to the vaulted cave walls and spindly, Victorian-looking lampposts. We're in the market district, surrounded by closed shops, boarded up or with windows smashed. Graffiti covers the walls. Only a couple of shops are in business, their neon signs half broken so only some of the letters light. Two figures in the foreground, perhaps silhouettes or perhaps only half in frame. This frame takes up the width of the page, but perhaps only a third of its height.

CAP: THE WARRENS. A NATION UNDERGROUND.

CAP: THE ROCKY RIBCAGE OF THE PLANET ASP.

2. This panel takes up the rest of the page, with the heroes taking up the space. **Rose** and **Flid** are standing before the door, bathed in the light of the pharmacy. They're dressed in something punky, perhaps. Maybe Flid wears a gasmask. Whatever, they look like they mean business. Flid's breasts show up through per shirt but per wears a codpicce as well. They're armed to the teeth, holding massive, crude-looking assault cannons. **Rose** wears either goggles or sunglasses.

ROSE: YOU READY?

FLID: ALWAYS.
LINKED: LET'S KICK ASS, BABE.

ROSE: (thought bubble) I COULD SMELL THE REEK OF BLEACH AND MEDICINAL ALCOHOL BEFORE WE EVEN STEPPED INSIDE. NEEDS DO AS NEEDS MUST.

PAGE 2.

1 Rose and Flid burst through the doors and point their weapons at the clerks stacking row upon row of medication. Nervous faces look up at the heroes, mouths ajar and eyes wide. Rose's gun is right in front of the nearest clerk, her bayonet touching the soft flesh beneath his chin.

ROSE: YOU! FILL UP THAT TROLLEY. TRANQS, MORPHINE, PIT LILY . . . GIVE US THE BEST STUFF YOU GOT AND NO ONE GETS HURT!

1 The clerks are filling up the trolley with as many drugs as they can. One of the clerks has his arms full of chems, which he's nervously dropping on the floor as he stumbles over to the trolley.

ROSE: (off panel) GIVE US THE BEST STUFF YOU GOT AND

NO ONE GETS HURT!

1 Rose and Flid flee the building, spilling pills everywhere as they race down the street, coasting along on the trolley's wheels. Rose is laughing and Flid has per arm around her waist, per hand sliding down towards Rose's arse.

1 They stop the trolley with their heels at a battered sports car further down the street. It is a red convertible type with the top down. A homeless man looks up from the doorway he's sleeping in, one cybernetic eye half in shadow beneath his hat.

1 Rose tips the contents of the trolley into the backseat of the sports car, bending forward provocatively, and Flid is pulling per mask off to reveal an androgynous, youthful face. Rose is half bent over the trunk of the car, her knees meeting in the middle, striking a classic Japanese schoolgirl pose. But from the knowing look on her face, we know this is purely for Flid's benefit. She's no docile bottom.

This became:

> Underground. Outside Sindar's Pharmacy. Light pours from the spindly iron lampposts and dies again mere feet away. We're in the market district, surrounded by closed shops — buildings boarded up or with windows smashed. Graffiti covers the walls. Only a couple of places are still in business, their neon signs half broken so only some of the letters light up in half-understood promises. Our shadows are silhouetted against the door like crooked fangs, hungry for what's inside.
>
> This, just one of the many eldritch streets worming like intestines through the rocky ribcage of the planet Asp. And we, just two of the thug-punk fuck-ups desperate to survive on a diet of cannibalism and through days of indentured slavery.
>
> Flid's wearing a gasmask, per features hidden in the

sadomasochistic gesture of rubber and tubing, like some elephant god twisted in the forges. Makes it hard to see per carved jawline, per elevated cheeks. Look down a bit and per breasts rook up the front of per shirt, and down more, per cock bulges ridiculously within a piratical codpiece. A perfect yin-yang, alchemical lover, to fuck and be fucked, here with per assault cannon. Per's got my back.

I wipe condensation from my goggles and nod at Flid. 'You ready?'

'Always.' Per smiles. 'Let's kick ass, babe.'

I can smell the reek of bleach and medicinal alcohol before we even step inside. Needs do as needs must.

Bursting through the door, we take the clerks by surprise, shoving our crude-looking cannons in their nervous faces. Row after row of medication spans the walls around us. My gun is right in front of the nearest clerk, my bayonet touching the soft flesh beneath his chin.

'You! Fill up that trolley. Tranqs, morphine, pit lily . . . Give us the best stuff you got and no one gets hurt!'

They begin scurrying round each other like battery hens on deformed ankles, filling their arms with chems and stumbling over to the trolley.

Within less than a minute the trolley's full. Packs of Narco-Sleep, Ibu-REM, Paradol, Crave-U-Want. Jars of brown herbs, silver leaves and purple grasses. Flid pops the door back open and I dash out, trolley clutched firmly in front of me like a plough. Spilling pills everywhere, we race down the street, coasting along on the trolley's wheels. Giggling like we're still the kids we used to be, picking food from the trash and sleeping in cracks under bridges or down fallen mine shafts. Flid wraps an arm around my waist, slides it down to the arch of my backside. I feel warm.

When we reach the end of the street, we stop the juggernaut with our heels, feeling the gravel beneath burn the rubber of our soles as we swing the trolley parallel to the battered sports car waiting for us. It's one of those red convertible types with the top down, waiting for us.

> Nearby a homeless man looks up from the doorway he's sleeping in, one cybernetic eye half in shadow beneath his hat. I flick him a grin full of shark teeth, turn and tip the contents of the trolley into the backseat of the car. Flid pulls off per mask and slings it onto the passenger's seat and we unsling the cannons from our backs, me bent over the trunk of the car, knees meeting in the middle, striking the vulnerable schoolgirl pose. And I know Flid's eyes are on my back, my arse, legs, the hair falling about my ears. Per knows I'm teasing; I'm no bottom. So per spanks me, playfully, and I jump up, chuckling, cheeks turning a soft pink.

As you can see, the latter is more fleshy, less skimpy than the naked body of the original, but pimps directly from the script to maintain the exhibitionism and keep things flowing quick, wet and ready.

Next in the development of the novella was the website. We took the artwork, gave it to Creative Director of Dog Horn Publishing (Michael Dark), and he created an interactive Flash-based website perfect for cyber-fraternising. This peep-show was somewhat tantalising: as though slowly revealing snippets of the book's flesh, teasing, to prolong the build-up of electric charge until the final release would see a big wad of British spec fic spunk right in your face.

Troglodyte Rose is a threesome: the prose, the art and the website. Together these build a multimedia text in constant fluid exchange with its rutting, coupling organs, and which, I hope, lends itself to a digital age with whorish audiences, attention spans equivalent to premature ejaculations, and a need for constant, guilt-free, no-strings-attached stimulus. As a result, the provocative limited edition pretty much sold out on the launch day. It then got nominated for two Lambda Awards and made it to the finals in the Transgender category for its intersex/hermaphrodite character, Flid. Now it has been tarted up, again, as a novel, which should make the *Trog Rose* text accessible to another kind of reader, who prefers his hookers to call themselves wives and wants them to stick around for something more long-term. This is the kind of literary prostitution Kathy Acker would be proud of.

These kinds of sticky interstices have been explored in other areas of my work, too. Take for example my recent post as writer in residence at the local I Love West Leeds Arts Festival. Visitors to Armley Mills, where the festival was centred, were pumped SMS poetry into their inboxes and I regaled children with tales of gay men cruising for cock in the car park outside. People could keep these texts like festering little infections or pass them on to friends like any good viral load, and many of them perhaps wouldn't have been exposed to my perversity otherwise.

I also kept an online journal of work throughout the residency, which included poetry, blogs and other literary masturbations. Readings of my work were recorded for the titillation of local radio and an interactive poetry map of West Leeds was created to encourage visitors to the website to click with their mouses among chants of 'Quicker, harder, faster!'.

The residency culminated in a poetry tour, which was filmed for next year's festival with all the grace of a skinflick, and was an entertaining free-for-all orgy between locals, poets and tourists. Unexpected additions to the tour (such as rapping MCs pulling up in a sports car, showing us what they could do with their tongues, then offering to sell us crack cocaine live on camera) made the experience much more than words splashed on a page ever could have.

Poetry and short stories are now being presented as slippery podcasts by websites such as Poetry Jukebox and PoetCasting.co.uk. There are cross-fucked events like Literary Death Match and Polari (London's gay literary salon), and we're witnessing the growing hard-on of the ebook coming at us, where it wants to spray its contents right in our eyes. I think it's only a matter of time before we're having cybersex with Mr D'Arcy and exploring interspecies love in a virtual reality based on the works of Burroughs.

Adam Lowe is a writer and publisher from Leeds, UK. In 2009 he received four Lambda Award nominations and three British Fantasy Award nominations. In 2008 he was awarded a Spectrum Fantastic Arts Award and he was 2010 writer in residence at the I Love West Leeds Arts Festival. His debut novella, *Troglodyte Rose*, was released to critical acclaim worldwide. He also writes for *Bent* magazine and *The Pink Paper*. His work has appeared in *Ex Plus Ultra*, *Unlikely Stories*, *The Cadaverine*, *Chimeraworld 5*, *The Leeds Guide*, *WAMACK*, *Saucytooth's* and PoetCasting.co.uk.

Maurice Stoker

Digital Warfare:
Interview with a Spy

From the vantage of Europe a different perspective on the terrorist threat emerges. Decidedly different. The vista grows more revealing the farther one removes oneself from the friendly centers of gravity of the "war," to put it in the jargon of the modern military. This being a so-called nonlinear conflict, it behooves the reviewer of this conflict to stand midway between the centers of gravity of the opposing sides.

Attempt to do so; what you find is that you cannot find the enemy's centers of gravity. Oh, there was a cleanup in Afghanistan, which is now more or less on its own. And then there is the slight-of-hand in Iraq, a place that never was a center of gravity though was certainly sold as such. In fact, Iraq was seen more as a way station in a move to find a leverage point for all the enemy (read Middle Eastern Islamic) centers of gravity. Whether this was a terrible misreading is yet to be decided; only time will tell. It is certainly is a test of certain theories of warfare, as the interviewee will reveal.

And in the US, where does one find the centers of gravity? Was the World Trade Center a center of gravity? Not really. It had no military significance in any meaningful sense. Yet it was indeed a center of gravity, in another sense. As was the Pentagon, even though some who understand the history of warfare would claim that destroying the Pentagon would actually help the US win wars. Bureaucrats running wars is a bad idea, and the Pentagon is nothing if not a hive for bumbling bureaucrats.

All this by way of introduction to our interview. The subject is the war on terrorism, as seen by a US spy, a field operative here in Europe. The interviewee perforce must remain in the limbo of anonymity; we call him K.

MS: By way of introduction, can you tell us something about yourself?

K: No.

MS: Then it would seem we have already met an impasse.

K: Abstractly speaking I'm a virtual warrior. Not always, though. Attended the finest war colleges in the world . . . including those in the US. But my specialty is nonlinear information warfare. I command a segment of that front from Europe.

MS: By virtual warrior, you don't mean to say that you don't exist in a corporeal sense.

K: Maybe. Can you see me?

MS: Can you explain a little about nonlinear warfare?

K: A little. It's a load of manure. There's no such thing. Or else it's a triviality. Pinheads who teach such bullflop like to point to the battle of Lodz in 1914 as an example in classical times. But the North Vietnamese general Giap taught us more about it beginning in 1968 with his distributed methods. Everyone thinks Vietnam was guerilla warfare, but it wasn't. Was light infantry acting in a distributed fashion, which is what the Army likes to call nonlinear in its operational doctrine of "AirLand warfighting." Except Giap had no air component. And the U S Army acted liked they were fighting WWII, which cost them the war without losing the battles. Or so it seemed. Mostly nonlinear means that troops are not stretched along a line, except by communications. Which is dangerous for centralized operations unless you can guarantee secure communications, as we learned in Vietnam thanks to the Walkers.

MS: You mean the spy ring led by John Walker.

K: Staffed by military personnel who sold codes used by ground troops. No telling how many died from that asshole's greed.

MS: Back to the topic. What are centers of gravity?

K: Fancy name for infrastructure, or headquarters, or sometimes just a way to break the will. These goons like to sound scientific, but they aren't even near science in this. It's old, this idea, but no one talked about it in the old days like they were scientists. When we bombed German railroads or factories in WWII, we were attacking centers of gravity, either directly or by cutting off their supply lines. When we firebombed Tokyo to demoralize the Japanese or wiped out electricity and other necessities in the Balkans under Clinton, we were doing the same. The will of the nation to continue is a center of gravity. Besides having hard value as infrastructure, these centers of gravity can have highly symbolic value. So the 911 attacks made the US look weak and al-Qaeda strong.

MS: Didn't that backfire?

K: Depends on the goal. I don't think it did, since it was a good step toward starting a radical Islamic uprising in the Middle East. Remember that that the schools where radical Islam is taught, where hatred of the US and Western culture is taught, like the schools in Pakistan, is one center of gravity. Though they're dispersed in space, it's still a center of gravity . . . a powerful point of difficulty for our handful of allies in Pakistan . . . prevents us flexing military muscle there. Iran's similar. Our hope is indiscriminant killing of Muslim civilians all over the region by terrorists counters these strengths . . . blows up in the faces of the perpetrators.

MS: An apt analogy. So then what do you think is the strategy in the war on terrorism? Is it a nonlinear type approach?

K: Course not. There's no real strategy in this so-called war on terror. In fact, there's no war on terrorism.

MS: I don't think I understand. The President claims we are at war.

K: In a formal way, we are at war. There's been a document signed that the President can claim is a declaration of war. Course, his claim's so broad this war could be engaged against any nation he doesn't like. And it could go on as long as the White House wants to use it as an excuse to extend its authority. But I leave that to the lawyers to sort out.

In a real sense, we're not hardly at war. There's no real battlefield except Iraq . . . the only place the Army doctrine's being tested. The war in Afghanistan is meaningless, since we either have to stay there forever or it reverts to warlords. But Iraq is all or nothing . . . a gamble with a huge chance of blowing up in our faces.

MS: How is this test being conducted in Iraq?

K: Consider the four tenets of Army doctrine as applied to low-intensity warfare. These are what Chesty Puller called small wars . . . fought in Nicaragua in the 1920s . . . which came to be distilled in the Marine Corps *Small War Manual.* Army could've used 'em in Vietnam, but they chose not to. Now they're applying it in Iraq, though they aren't admitting it. In fact, they've modified it into a new doctrine, which they consider tailored to using technology to reduce troop levels . . . so-called force multipliers. Sometimes technology's a crock . . . like when the Serbs fooled our heat seekers by setting bonfires. After our bombardment did nothing but stir up dirt . . . next day we found out we hadn't damaged their armor or their troops or anything but a bunch of trees.

MS: Could you expand on this for us?

K: In principle it's a four step program . . . we can apply it to all war types, including low intensity conflict like Iraq. First step's intelligence study and analysis of potential battlefield. This was done poor in Iraq . . . filtered through delusional ideology . . . saw it as a conventional war ending in the hero worship and adulation of the WWII liberations of Europe.

This step hasn't even been taken in the so-called war on terror.

Second step's to establish conditions for dominance of the battle area . . . gain and keep the initiative. Course, that's always the goal . . . nothing new. In low-intensity conflicts like Iraq it should involve training friendly forces, whatever that means with the proliferation of religious militias. Unfortunately, in Iraq that step failed completely because the military thought that by defeating Saddam's military it had been accomplished. Stupids in control, so to speak. People like to point to the Vietnam debacle as too many civilians micromanaging the war . . . tying the military's hands . . . but that's another crock of crybaby blubbering. Fact is, the Iraq fiasco's been far more micro-managed than Vietnam was . . . with the complicity of kiss-ass generals who worry more about keeping their jobs than the troops.

Third stage is operations, which sort of slipped up on us in Iraq. In fact, it was the Iraqi insurgents who chose when to begin this stage, not us. Supposedly this would be where the national elections . . . protected by those troops we never trained . . . elected a government of the people, etcetera. But with the sectarian split, that's an unlikely outcome. Course, we can debate the existence of a government of the people in the US, too, since from my vantage point the US governmental structure is pretty alienated from its citizens. There is a pronounced split, I think . . . one thing seems certain: all sides want to choose security over liberty . . . Probably old Ben Franklin's rolling over in his grave.

MS: He said that any people that chooses security over liberty deserves neither, or something to that effect.

K: He published a work saying any nation making such a choice deserved neither . . . . He didn't write it himself.

Anyway, forth stage'll be withdrawal of troops, maybe to invade Iran or Syria.

MS: I'd like for you to briefly expand on that statement about alienation of citizenry from the government.

K: Not all the citizens . . . not yet anyway. It's a gradual process. Right now the US is in the hands of Christian mullahs and ayatollahs who gained control of the election process at the primary level and at the PR level . . . twice elected a God-intoxicated President who casts the universe in black and white terms of good and evil. Fortunate for him, unfortunate for themselves . . . Americans being the most poorly educated and semiliterate and unable to reason of all the people in the industrialized world and not knowing it because they don't travel or read or work in difficult occupations requiring thought, which we fill with educated immigrants . . . they don't see it. Worse, being more superstitious than any third world country, a lot of 'em believe he does represent God and talks to God. He is truly a President of the Babbits, but the US has a larger proportion of Babbits now than it did in Sinclair Lewis's day. In fact, most Americans would aspire to be Babbits, and want nothing more for their kids . . . . But then Americans are perhaps the most cowardly people on earth.

MS: How do you mean cowardly?

K: Well, how many of these flag-waving patriots you see sending their kids to join up and fight? Army can't make recruiting goals without incredible bribery, and then the best get out fast as they can. And haven't you seen the shift in television commercials? Used to be, when I was a kid, they sold everything with sex. Now the citizens are too scared of AIDS and God or whatever to do sex, but they are scared of flu and infection and old age and heart attack and stroke and inability to retire without eating out of trash cans and car wrecks and getting lost in their cars and terrorists and God knows what else . . . every damned commercial plays to that fear. I don't see that anywhere else in the world.

MS: You sound kind of cynical.

K: You sound kinda stupid.

MS: So you say this doctrine is being tested in Iraq. How is that?

K: What're you? Stupid? We tested the same damned doctrine in Vietnam, though it hadn't been called that. We used it in WWII, Korea, every damned war there ever was. The bit about establishing a viable government is essentially the same as establishing a satrapy.

Where you been? You really think this is about fighting a ragged band of terrorists who found one of the multitude of holes in our porous national security?

MS: If that isn't what it is, then what is it?

K: A war on the liberty of the citizens of the US by the religious nuts running the country. Only the citizens don't really understand it. This is about government taking more control.

MS: You mean by pushing constitutional powers of the President over the powers of the judicial and the legislative branches of government?

K: That whole separation of powers thing's been a crock from the beginning. Don't forget the US was started by a bunch of angry white men . . . all property owners . . . who hated to pay taxes. The high sounding words about freedom and liberty and all that was pure nonsense. I mean, women didn't have the right to vote until the 20th century. And worse yet, that bit about all men created equal in a country full of slaves? Black slaves? And slave-owners like Washington planning to steal land from the Indians? Were they equal? Maybe they weren't men . . . .

And now Antonin Scalia holds seances with Clarence Thomas . . . which is why he wasn't nominated as Chief Justice . . . soon maybe the two new nuts'll join 'em . . . to find out how these dead white men would return our century to theirs.

MS: You don't sound like someone who ought to be defending our national security interests.

K: Why? I am part of a sizeable minority within the community living on the taxpayers in exchange for national security. Some are better compensated than others. We mostly do it for the money, dude. I am very well compensated. Plus the fact is I get to live in a free country somewhere in Europe. It's no surprise lots of us want to work Europe . . . want to retire in Europe. The US is not a free country, particularly now that the religious nuts are running it. And it's gonna get worse.

MS: I guess I am a bit confused by what you are saying.

K: My job has several aspects. One of them is keep tabs on some low-level terrorist threats and if possible, divert them to European targets. Preferably away from where I reside. Another is to help the executive branch scare the shit out of the lily-livered American public so they can gain more and more control. But that's easy, as cowardly as the citizens of the US happen to be. Another is . . .

MS: Wait. You are making certain that the Administration has materials to frighten the country into granting powers to the President?

K: Sure. This last tape of Bin Laden's was an obvious fake. The Arabic was not in his style at all. And yet on every damned news interview they accredited that to his being surrounded by non-Arabic speakers. People swallowed that? Come one. He's the only one needing to speak Arabic. Shit, you think he had a bunch of damned speech writers? Someone said it was because he was surrounded by English speakers. That's true, in a sense.

MS: You mean Bin Laden works for us?

K: No. The man lives in a computer. There's no difficulty synthesizing his speech, given the tapes we have in possession. That's a triviality. We can synthesize any speech we want . . . make it sound just like him. Make it BE him. We even create completely synthetic films of him and his deputies . . . cartoons so realistic no one could tell they aren't real. We're a hell of a lot more advanced than Pixar.

MS: But we can't write in his style.

K: That's right. We can't write in his style . . . we know it. We tried and it turned out to be garbage. That was the prior tape. So now we don't try.

MS: But we know he's dead and we don't tell the American public?

K: You are naïve. Would you want your kids to know the bogeyman was a myth?

MS: How do you know this tape was faked? From the circumstantial evidence of the style on the latest tape?

K: No. I am part of a team to get these fake tapes into the al-Qaeda channel so that everyone knows it came from Bin Laden.

MS: You mean . . .

K: I mean I run the network that delivers it into the chain of al-Qaeda operatives. We infiltrated that bunch of rag heads ages ago, before Clinton.

MS: Well, this is at best unsettling. Why would the government want to gain more control over its citizens?

K: Isn't that a typical pattern? Particularly when the bidness boosters gain control . . . their entire lives are devoted to being control freaks. The whole philosophy of bidness administration is based on how good it is to be a control freak on top of the dung heap. The rest is just fancy words.

MS: So you work with the administration to take away individual liberty?

K: Sure. It's a job. Public service is an oxymoron. And meantime . . . seeing what's happening in the homeland . . . a lot of us look for ways out. That was why the punishment for the station chief in Italy . . . the one who got caught kidnapping people they thought might be terrorists . . . you remember? . . . was so ironic.

MS: Ironic?

K: Sure. They put out a warrant for his arrest to Interpol, in Europe. Now he can't return to Europe. He'd just retired. He had a nice villa in Italy. That was where he was going to spend his golden years. Now he can't set foot in Europe. That sort of vengeance scares all of us. We could end up forced to live in the prison camp called the United States of America. Ironic, huh? We help build and secure the prison . . . then end up forced to live in it.

MS: Do these messages from Bin Laden serve any other purpose?

K: Not just from Bin Laden, but from almost the entire crew. A lot of what is happening in Iraq to certain citizens . . . blamed on terrorists . . . is us or the Brits. Not all of course . . . we don't kill our own troops, at least not intentionally. Just to stir up sectarian shit. But it's true these bin Laden tapes are coded messages . . . except the messages are meant to for our operatives working inside the various centers of gravity we've infiltrated.

MS: Can you give us an example?

K: Nothing beyond our infiltration of al-Qaeda. It'd be giving up too much.

MS: It seems you've already given up too much.

K: Nothing they don't know and the US public won't believe. After all, they pay more than any other nation in the industrialized world for the worst health care in the industrialized world. They are so stupid they consider the right to vote synonymous with liberty and freedom. There are plenty of dictatorships that offer more freedom and individual liberty than democracies. Democracy can be incredibly tyrannical. The tyranny of the masses. Ask a black slave living in the south before abolition. That was a democracy.

MS: So are you concerned about the loss of personal information?

K: Of course. But some of us have methods to defeat the NSA net that actually sieves every phone call into or out of the US . . . no matter where it's going or where it came from. It's not simple. It's far easier to defeat their email nets. No matter what technology you develop, there's a work around. The Serbs understood that.

But the stupidest thing people say is I don't care. I got nothing to hide. Only a moron says that. Everybody's got something to hide . . . the man who truly has nothing to hide will be crucified with an invention . . . just like happened to Jesus Christ . . . that metaphorical scapegoat. Any nation that can trash its veterans and war heroes while praising as heroes cowardly men who ran and hid from their national duty is capable of anything. As Franklin said, Any nation that trades liberty for security deserves neither.

MS: That's a repetition, and I don't think Franklin himself said it.

K: Yes, I said that earlier . . . I think you're right . . . he only published it. But I'm sure he believed it. He is one founding father people don't pay attention to. Another's Jefferson. Christ, Pat Buchanan claimed he wished George Washington had established a monarchy. But then the so-called conservative movement is a crock . . . small government . . . strong defense . . . they can't occur simultaneously. Whenever the small government crowd gets in power watch out . . . they always create the biggest, nosiest, most invasive governments. Assholes . . . it's why Hayek wrote the essay about why he wasn't a conservative.

MS: Well, thanks for your disquieting comments. It will give us plenty to think about.

K: No one'll believe it except those who already know it . . . for all you know this may have been orchestrated by Them for some nefarious purpose.

MS: Which would be?

K: I'm done here.

Maurice Stoker is a professor of mathematical literature at the Open University of The European Union with a quasi-endowed lectureship at the College de France where he replaced Michel Foucalt as the school open butthole. He specializes in the techniques of best selling literature, having demonstrated mathematically that what sells is "tell, don't show", and not the "show, don't tell" espoused by agents, editors and others known to have their heads up their asses.

Though proudly queer as a three-dollar bill, Maurice admits to having been married at one time to a holy slut named Anastasia, rumored to be the incarnation of Krunga Legpa'i Zangpo. As an adept, Anastasia's goal is to fuck or otherwise sexually satisy all sentient and most quasi-sentient beings. She was particularly fond of Maurice's German shepherd guard dogs, which is said to have been the inspiration for the classic Japanese zoophilia film Dog Rape starring Rinako Hirasawa. The 'byang chub sems dpa' Anastasia felt so much empathy for so many horny beings that she is the patron saint of the now defunct Clube Bahamas in Sao Paulo, Brazil. She is sometimes confused with Suzy Creamcheese, which Maurice says this is a result of media mistaking Anastasia for Lady Creamhair. It has also been falsely reported that the incarnation of Krunga Legpa'i Zangpo is Catherine Millet, though it is well known that Millet is the incarnation of Sahajayogin?cint?. Maurice was so devestated when Anastasia ran off with a male goat that he subsisted for a month on a diet of male semen while confined to a glory hole. Even this is said to have been a reflection of his jealousy of his divine wife who is said to have existed for twenty years on nothing more than male seminal fluid.

Nowadays besides teaching, Maurice helps market writing by leading service tours of glory holes. He recently led a tour with of the US that included Bush the Younger and his former Vice Dick Cheney, mostly to truck stops and interstate rest stops. But his most important work is in literary software, which is replacing human authors. Parameter driven, this software emulates any number of styles, with the ability to blend styles, and can generate both fiction and nonfiction and works in-between. There are a number of best sellers now on the market that are the product of the software. The only difficulty is that it is possible to generate dozens of novels in a matter of minutes under the banner of a single author, whereas now most popular authors only produce a dozen or so works per year.

Harold Jaffe

Manson:
Even the Devil — If there is a Devil — Had a Beginning

Dr. Pepper

My ma's younger brother was named Luther Kinlock. He lived in West Virginia, which is where we moved from Ohio when I was not even a year old. Luther didn't have no kind of real job so him and Kathleen — my ma — they decided to rob a gas station in Charleston, West Virginia. What they used as a weapon was a full bottle of Dr. Pepper which they tried to hit the attendant on the head with, but they messed up and got nabbed.

First rape

Bennett Home for Boys. Clarksburg, West Virginia. I was ten years old, the youngest, smallest kid in the joint. Seven, eight bigger kids — they gang-raped me. When I got it together to go to the assistant superinten-dent, mo'fucker called Fish, he told me pull my pants down, bend over and show where they got me. When I did he spit tobacco juice on his hand and shoved it up my ass. Then he says to the guard: "Okay, he's primed, let them fuck his brains out."

I never got a chance to even things up with Fish, but that night at about three a.m. I took a window crank — one of them steel rods that push open or pull shut the windows. Was about sixteen inches long and about three pounds. I went to the bunk of the first dude that fucked my ass and hit him eight or nine blows hard as I could hit to the head and face. About killed him. Too fuckin' bad I dint.

Father Flanagan's Boys Town

They sent my ass there after I busted out of Bennett. But I busted out of Flanagan after like four days, me and some other kids. Stole cars and broke into stores an' shit. Even held up one old guy and slapped him around a little bit. They caught us four days later. Sent me to Prideaux Juvenile Detention in Indiana, which was raunchy. But I wasn't 'bout to do no time at no Father Motherfucker's Boys Town.

Pelican Bay

Where I'm at now? Ain' no biggie. Tomorrow — if I'm alive — they could transfer me to some other hard-ass joint, you dig?

How many state and federal joints I been in my life, dog? Ain' nothin' changed. No, no, no, no. Negativity, man. If I ask for a bucket of shit they're like: No fuckin' way, Manson.

Truth is they'd ruther see me dead. 'Cept they afraid the fuckin' consequence. Still folks out there love my ass. If they don't love me, they need me, you dig? Most the other big-time devil soundbites are dead and gone: Hitler, Nixon, Bundy, John Wayne Gacy, Che Guevara.

Me, I'm at world's end, shackled, sensory deprived, under 24/7 surveillance, but I'm Charles mo'fuckin' Manson, evil incarnate, you dig?

Death Valley

I dreamt of the desert but never seen it till, what?, '67. Was love at first sight, dog. Plus I'm a quick study. It I wasn't I wouldna made it this far.

Coyote

Jesus crucified. You ever see a coyote move? He's rhythm and grace. He's aware of everything that's in motion because it's either prey or something gonna prey on him. You listen close for a long time to the coyote and you gonna hear just about every sound there is — howl, bark, growl, yip, wail, whistle. The coyote is total fear, total paranoia, which is what you must have to survive on this fucked-over planet. Yet he's relaxed, delicate in all his movements, at peace in his total fear that never ends. If a coyote is ever in trouble or captured he will do whatever it takes to get free, bite off his own tail or leg, even change identities, like become a sidewinder or a crow. That's why the Indians call him Trickster. If I was an animal I'd be a coyote. If I wasn't a coyote I'd be a scorpion.

Rommel in the desert

Yeah, I was gonna have my tribe raid some the neighboring towns, turn all them born-agains into anti-capitalist hippies.

Rommel in the desert, Buddha in the desert, Jesus in the desert. I had all kinds of shit in mind one time or 'nother. You drop acid a bunch your mind gets to zoomin'. Mostly, I just wanted to be left alone with my coyotes and scorpions and geetar. I never made no big deal out of it. I was livin' in the desert. You all done come and git me, remember? I was happy doin' what I'm doin'.

Vincent Bugliosi

Dude wanted to gas as much of the Manson family as he could get his hands on, you dig? He'd be right there in the execution chamber, first row, jackin' off in his head.

There I was on Death Row in Quentin kinda looking forward to the gas. But after that ACLU challenge went to the Supreme Court they postponed then commuted all the pending executions. Had nothing to do with compassion, you dig? Was a legal thing. This country of yours ain' into no compassion for po' folks.

Like I said, I didn't give a shit either way, but not executing Manson broke Bugliosi all up, I thought he was like to weep.

You got to understand that beneath Bugliosi's DA swagger he was a puss. In that lyin' book he got rich on, he has me so mojo powerful that just remembering one my stares would stop his pissing midflow.

The Manson stare

It's simple, basic voodoo. Like me starin' at you now. You see how I'm starin' at you? Answer me, dog.

I see

Cool. Now you go home and try to fuck your wife, you ain' gonna be able. Just lookin' at you I can see that your sex life wasn't worth shit to begin wit'. But I just wrecked what was left of it for all time.

Voodoo

Thas right. I'm in Pelican Bay State Penitentiary, 68-years-old, shackled, sensory deprived, under constant surveillance, but I'm Charley Manson, you dig. So folks send me stuff, presents, neckties, socks, sweaters. But I ain' no clothes horse and never was. Naked and dick swinging's my deal. So what I do with my hands cuffed is unravel the ties and socks and sweaters and tank tops 'n shit and make voodoo dolls. I make scorpions and cockroach cages too.

[laughs] My dolls done murdered and maimed some bad-ass human mo'fuckers. You know as well as me some folks ain' fit to live.

Manson orgies on video

[laughs] Yeah, we shot a lot of fim and vid. Plus other folks — visitors and such — they shot us. We looked good and we knew how to fuck and suck. Ever'body wanted a piece of us. Some the fims we ourselves took we swapped for dope. The other fims — I know where they're at, and they're hot.

Yo! dog, get my ass sprung from Pelican Bay and I'll make sure you be doin' a whole lot of jackin' off to Manson and his family. [laughs]

Hand signals

My hands move in the direction of my blood. You wouldn't understand the principle of that.

God of fuck

Got Bugliosi all worked up. That's 'cuz he's a tight-ass career-sucking opportunist that don't even know what it means to fuck. I said I was the god of fuck to Lynette Squeaky Fromme first time I done her. Underneath a great old Redwood. Go ask Squeaky how she liked it. Go ask all my other sweet-smelling girls. They was sweet-smelling back then. Cain't say how they smell now the Law has got in their panties.

Sadie Mae Glutz

Shot off her mouth in jail. Sold some made-up story to one of the weeklies. Copped a plea before the grand jury. Became a quote-unquote born-again. That's what she claimed anyway. Bought her some pity, but didn't get her ass sprung.

Before she joined up with the family she was a devil worshiper with what's his face up there in San Francisco. LaVey. Mindfuck was her thing. Whatever Sadie was into Sadie wanted to be top dog, you dig? Fucking included. With me that never happened, you dig? After I balled her inside out and sideways, she done cried like a little girl. She'd go on 'bout how I was God. Which is dog spelled backwards.

Like some people, they say Sadie's gorgeous and sexy. You know what? Even the bulldykes in Frontera, where she's at, they won't go near her. She's toxic. I never dug Sadie Mae Glutz, never trusted her even back when she called herself Susan Atkins. She even smelled raunchy. Her skin, her hair.

Kashmir Clap

[laughs] That's a Sadie deal, right? If Sadie caught the clap she done caught it outside the family. She'd spread for anything that farted.

How many young folks moving through the family did I fuck? Eight hundred? Thousand? Not a one of 'em ever had the Kashmir clap or the Timbuktu clap to my knowledge. And I reckon I'd be the mo'fucker to know.

Nature lover, vegetarian

That's me. Just like Gandhi.

Just like Hitler

I ain' got nuffin' 'gainst Hitler, dog. Hitler's coo'. Monster like me. That's what yawl made me. You fear me and you want to fuck me. Ain't that why you got all hotted up about the fims was shot of the family orgies?

Where are the films at, Charlie? How can I get my doggy paws on 'em? How can I slobber all over them with my forked tongue?

Haight-Ashbury

It's 1967 and I just finished up a 15-year deal at Terminal Island, a fed joint near San Pedro. I told 'em I didn't want to leave and they laughed at me. Bunch of murders and mayhem later [laughs], they wish they done kept my ass inside.

Takes me a little while get my shit together, then I go up to the Haight because I hear that's where the cool runnings is at. I play my geetar, right? The fems just keep comin'. Mary Brunner — she was a librarian at the University of San Francisco medical school. I was pickin' on the street near Golden Gate Park, my black watch cap on the pavement for spare change. I see Mary Brunner walking her boxer, dog shit bag in her hand, nose in the air, and I say real soft, "Babe, listen to this yere melody. I play it just for you." She stopped, I played the song. Bang.

Mary was the first of the so-called Manson family. I called her Mercy and gave her the color blue. Then came Squeaky, which is what we called Lynette Fromme. I gave her the color green. Then came fucked-up Susan Atkins. Then Katie Krenwinkle, and Simi Valley Sheri. And Sandy Good.

It was getting crowded, you dig, so I scammed a school bus, painted it black. We rode from the Haight up and down the coast, into Utah, Nevada, then back down to LA, pickin' up girls at ever' stop. Once in a while there'd be a dude.

Manson does dudes?

Sho. I'm 68 years old and been in prison 56 years. Ain' no girls in prison that I know of.

Was one male, pastor father of Ruth Ann Moorehouse. Ouisch we called her. She was like 14 when she got on the Manson bus outside of Flagstaff, I think it was. Man, could she fuck. Well, by the time we got to LA her old man, Pentecostal pastor from Broken Arrow, Oklahoma, where Ouisch run away from — old man Moorehouse was waitin' on me with another dude, great big shaved-head mo'fucker packin' a semi-automatic. Desert Eagle 10-mm, if I remember correct.

No biggie. Problem solving is what I excel at, you dig? I sweet-talked them a little, fixed the shaved-head loon up with two my girls, then took a private walk with the preacher, slipped him some acid, and fucked him in the ass. You know that these Pentecostals talk in tongues, right? Well, this dude, Ouisch's old man out of Broken Arrow, Oklahoma, was squealin' in tongues while I was punkin' him. That's how much he loved my dick in his ass, you dig?

I dint feel the same way. Was like stickin' my fist in a sewer drain.

After that, "Preacher" was one my most loyal followers. Till he died a year or so later.

Submit

You and honkies like you cain't see that these hundreds of young humans that joined my family were humans that you all abandoned, humans alongside the road that, when they wouldn't eat their cheese-burgers, their parents kicked them out or tried to stick them in Juvenile Hall. So I done the Christian thing and took them in and told them that in love there was no wrong. All they had to do was give up the lies and bad shit they learned and submit. Submission. Did I submit my own self? Damn right. You can't enjoy fucking or even getting stoned if you don't submit.

Anger and rage

My ma dropped me when she was 16 and a ho cuz she was an illiterate Appalachian hillbilly. I never knew my father. We scrambled from town to town. I done 7 years for a 37 dollar check. I done 12 years because I was piss-poor without no parents. I was gang-raped in reform school when I was ten years old. Yeah, dog, I had anger and rage.

How's anyone not going to have anger and rage living in what they done turned this sweet world into?

Mystical hole in Death Valley

What was down the hole it ain' for honkies like you all to know. But I'll say this. I found a hole that goes down to a river that runs north underground. I called it a bottomless pit because where could a river be flowing north underground? Was so wide and deep you could even sail a ship on it. Was no penal institutions and TV down there. So I covered it up and called it "The Devil's Hole," and we all laughed and joked about it.

Black folks

Ever since I shot that big wannabe Black Panther spade Lotsapoppa in '69, I think it was, people, even so-called Manson experts, been sayin' I have trouble with blacks and such, but it ain' no truth to it. Lotsapoppa ripped me off in a drug deal. He coulda been French or Chinese and I still woulda shot his ass. Black dint have nothin' to do with it.

Like Lamar Duane Cady, we called him Fang, the Skull Helmet biker that lived on the movie ranch, he hated blacks, and when he'd rap with me I'd like nod my head. So he'd go away sayin': Charlie agrees with me. But I was just reflectin' back what he hisself thought.

Yo, I been in prison all my life, and that's the first thing you learn: go wit' the flow 'less you're big enough and shit-eating enough to bust some heads. See, I ain' big, but I'm shit-eating.

You know what else I am? I'm a piss-poor hillbilly spend all my fuckin' life in prison. Prisons in damn near ever' city in this country of yours. And who's in these prisons of yours? Black folks and po' folks. A piss-poor hillbilly in the joint ain' nuffin' but a nigger.

Reflecting back

What I'm reflectin' back is this yere country we live in. Hypocrisy, lust in the head, xenophobia, cruelty to your brother. It ain't that I am or do these things, you dig, but that people — Christian family people like you all — see in me what's in their deepest selves but that they cain't bear to look at. That's why for so long I was the most famous face in all of capitalism.

Pimp Manson

Thas me. I was into a bunch of shit, you dig. And, yeah, pimpin' was one my thangs. An older con that ran with Bonnie and Clyde — he told me once there was nothing like turning a chick out. He was on the money, dog. Deep down every fem wants to be a ho. I was real good at seeing they got what they wanted. And it bought me time to set around, get stoned, do my music.

Punked in Quentin

'Nother lie makin' the rounds, that some Aryan Brotherhood dude made me his bitch when I was in Quentin in the early Seventies. Nobody done touched me inside since that time I was gang-raped as a kid. Well, this Pachuco gang doused me with paint thinner and lit me up. That was in Calipatria, by the border. I got some my hair and skin burned. No big deal. And three skanky Hare Krishna cons jumped me, but that was in Soledad. Anyway I kicked their asses all over the yard, the three of 'em.

The Krishnas thought I was dissing their Hindu jive. With the Mex gang it was Macho shit. I was a big target, okay? Light Manson up and get famous. Gonna take a lot more than Pachuco punks and skanky Krishnas to do me any real hurt.

Cocksman

[laughs] Yo lookin' at him.

Lotta folks ask me who was better, me or Cupid, Bobby Beausoleil. Lovin' good takes a good dick, but that ain' all. It's like the way innocent little kids play, every bit of the body alive. Me, I fired from all cylinders. At the same time I always took my time, knew just what the fem wanted. And I gave it to her. Just not all at once, you dig?

Yeah, the family girls loved Cupid's dick, and he knew how to use it. But after I copped him in the ass I owned him. He'd do anything I say.

Roman Polanski

A kind of ham. Polish ham

Dennis Wilson of the Beach Boys

I was waitin' on him at his mansion, it was like 2:30 am. As he pulled into the fancy driveway in his purple Ferrari I stepped out of the shadows. Dude saw me and was like: Please don't hurt me. I said: Do I look like I'm going to hurt you, brother? And I never did hurt him neither. Though some-times he gave me cause. He copped my music, you know, stuck it on one of his LP's, changed a few my lyrics and never gave me no credit for it.

Two-and-a-half incandescent years

I know where you're goin', dog, 'cuz other people — so-called Manson experts — come up with the exact same thing. The whole Manson family deal was between May '67 and December '69. We done a lifetime load of bad shit during that real short time.

So if I was offered a devil's bargain: two-and-a-half years, like what I had with my girls and sex and dope and Death Valley and those raunchy murders that I supposedly done or instigated — if I was offered them two-and-a-half years in exchange for spending the rest of my life in prison, would I take it?

You know what, dog, it took me a while to get in the groove. After doin' 15 years in Terminal Island I was on the streets a lot of days before I got my nuts out of hock. Once I found the groove, though, it done never stopped. And I ain' gonna lie to you: I enjoyed the ride.

'Cept close to the end, around the time the big murders — 'cuz there was some other murders folks still don't know about — close to the end, the shit turned. Was me callin' the shots and I let us slip into this end-of -the-world thing, diggin' up bunkers, storing water and supplies, keepin' a step ahead of the pigs that was out to nail us. All that Helter Skelter shit.

Family would look at me like, "What now, Charlie?" And I wasn't always able to tell' 'em. My creativity was like slipping. I guess it was that two-and-a-half year devil's pact comin' to an end.

But would I do it again, even if I knew on one side was prison and on the other side was prison? Yeah, I would. Because prison ain' that big a deal, dog. Jail sucks but it's my life.

Helter Skelter

Was a goof. Bunch of us on the movie ranch was stoned on acid and jivin' around. Someone, I think maybe Snake, come up with that Beatles White Album and we got to listenin' to it close, with the acid workin'. So we started messin' around with the "Revolution" lyrics an' shit. To DA Bugliosi, it was like: Revolution plus Beatles plus Manson = Big time $$$ for his own self. So he ran wit' it. He's full of poop. I could care less about the fuckin' White Album. I'm a hillbilly. Gimme Woody Guthrie. Gimme Hank Williams senior. Gimme early Dylan on acoustic.

Sharon Tate murders

Wasn't me that murdered her, dog. I didn't know her or the Polish ham that was her husband cuz I never did see none their flicks. Yeah, I hung out a little with actors 'n shit, and this one famous matinee idol — he's dead now and I won't say his name — paid me to fuck his ass. But I never mixed with no Sharon Tate and Polish ham.

Freaky shit, I like it

Sadie Mae Glutz said that when she tasted the blood off the knife she used to stab Sharon Tate in her pregnant belly. Sadie admitted it then denied it. But Tex Watson and Katy Krenwinkle both heard her say it.

Jesus Manson

You a church-going dog so maybe you know that before the church fathers got ahold of him, Jesus was an Essene, a hippy. He wore a jellaba, which is a long robe, with no underwear, not even a jock strap. What a family man like you would call an athletic supporter. He had long hair, and traveled with a bunch of long-haired followers. Apostles he called them. Ring a bell?

Manson of a thousand faces

You five-foot-three and in hard-ass penal institutions your whole damn life you learn to adjust or else you die. You puff up like Mike Tyson, you vibe out like Jesus, you squeeze and shrink and fade like road kill . . .

You a dog and a foo', but you got to understand just a little bit of this without my sayin'. Man, I sometimes wish they'd send me someone has some brain and maybe just a little bit of soul. But I reckon ain' too many like that out there. See, what you and your kind are is just what we was fightin' 'gainst back then. Rid the fuckin' earth of yawl.

You lost that fight

Wrong again. What you all think is lost has just gone underground. Like a desert plant, you dig? Could take another ten, twenty years for the right conditions then it will rise again faster than you can believe, all strong and prickly. Foo' like you put his hand on it come away poisoned and bloody.

Favorite mass-murderer excluding yourself

Finally you come up wit a question that ain' half-ass. Favorite mass-murderer excluding myse'f?

That would be Henry Kissinger. Madonna called him Caca. She was fuckin' him. You remember OJ, right? The Juice? Well, OJ'd 'd bang Madonna from behind while she doin' a strap-on number on Caca. Some-times she'd ram her fist up there. He liked it, Caca. His stretch limo would be waitin' outside Madonna's Park Avenue triplex. Was a regular occurrence, Madonna, OJ, Caca. This was way before the OJ trial.

OJ's guy, Johnny Cochran

Uh-huh. I sometimes think what if I had slick Johnny Cochran argue my case. Know what? I woulda fuckin' walked. I'd be back in the desert with the coyotes and scorpions fingerin' my geetar.

Provisional Final Words

Yo, I had my run. Two-and-a-half incandescent years. Ain't that the word you used: incandescent? Now I'm back inside where I belong. It's my home. Ever'body has to have some kinda home. Pelican Bay. Don't it have a nice sound? You know what I do in my solitary cell in Pelican Bay? I sit there thinking of nothing. Nothing to think about. If I could, I'd jerk this microphone out and beat your brains out with it, because that's what you and the rest yawl deserve. But I don't have none that anger and rage you was talkin' about. You're a scabby, housebroken old dog. A dumb, soulless motherfuckin' piece of shit wears a nametag and do just what they want you to do. You know how quick I could slit your belly, snatch out your liver? But do I want to get your pissy blood all over me? No, I don't. I most definitely don't. I'm just sittin' here wit' my shackled hands pickin' my imaginary geetar waitin' on some ties and socks and tee shirts that I can make voodoo dolls out of for all them upstanding Christian human beans out there in Freedomland.

NOTES:

*Multiple texts, online and off, constitute the raw material that I've re-imagined into my serial killer "docufictions." The Crime library, Melange, Angelfire, APBnews, as well as individual killers' home-pages are among the Web sites I read or glanced over; as well as too many hard copy volumes to cite in this space.

**"Dr Death" was published in a somewhat different format in my volume False Positive (FC2, 2002).

Harold Jaffe is the author of sixteen books, including nine fiction collections, four novels and two volumes of essays. Jaffe's fiction has appeared in many journals and has been anthologized in *The Pushcart Prize; Best American Stories; Best of American Humor,* and elsewhere. An issue of *The Journal of Experimental Fiction* called "The Literary Terrorism of Harold Jaffe" was devoted to his writings in 2004. Jaffe has been interviewed widely, in various countries. His novels and short fiction have been translated into German, Japanese, Spanish, Italian, French, Dutch, Czech, Farsi, and Serbo-Croatian. He has won two NEA grants in fiction, two Fulbright fellowships, California Arts Council fellowship in fiction, a San Diego fellowship (COMBO) in fiction, and three Pushcart Prizes in fiction. Jaffe is editor-in-chief of the literary/cultural journal *Fiction International.*

Jonathan Penton

Seen

One autumn, I looked into the mirror and could not recognize my face. My features seemed no more or less remarkable, just foreign. When I smiled, then frowned, then looked puzzled, my face took completely unfamiliar positions, unrelated to my intended expressions.

I was living in a garret, an elevated apartment attached to a residential estate in El Paso, Texas, about a mile north of the bridge into Cuidad Juarez, Chihuahua, Mexico. I lived in an historic neighborhood called Sunset Heights, a series of hills that offered a remarkable view of downtown El Paso and much of Juarez. The neighborhood was largely designed by Henry Trost, a student and contemporary of Frank Lloyd Wright; my landlord, Sherman, lived in the house that Trost himself had lived in. I lived in a plain, two-story brick building in the back of Sherman's property; the first story, his garage, I rented as my workshop, and I lived in the top story, which was presumably designed as maids' quarters.

In order to get to my apartment, I walked through a fantastic garden of curved pathways, palm trees, and rarely-functioning pixie lamps. I walked through a stately outer door; from there, my workshop was directly in front of me, and the dusty stairs to my apartment were to my left. Turning onto them, I passed a window overlooking the garden, which I kept open, and in which my cat preferred to spend her time when it was less than ninety degrees out. Another swing to the left would put you at my front door.

The apartment had no address, other than my landlord's, and if you didn't know it was back there, and didn't know I was living in it, you were very unlikely to stumble across it. When I was home, I would leave my apartment's door cracked open, and the outer door bolted. The garage had windows, and I would leave one of them open; it opened into an open-air storage facility in which Sherman stored things owned by his more outdoorsy relatives; I was fairly certain he had no idea what he was storing there. As a result, my cat had full access to my apartment and the neighborhood at all times, without the use of a pet door. If a thief knew the property fully, he or she would have no problem climbing through that window and getting into my workshop, where he or she would find many thousands of dollars worth of extremely heavy printing and binding equipment; while the machines were clearly expensive, neither the average thief nor the average pawnbroker would know what they were. Climbing the stairs, our raider would find easy access to a fairly impressive array of computer equipment and a large psychiatric patient drinking tequila and pacing from mirror to mirror.

My apartment had no interior walls save the one that led to the bathroom, but it did use support beams and a kitchen bar to subdivide space. Entering my apartment, I faced an 8'x10' area with a carpet that I had often stained. The room could be described as a foyer or dining nook; this had become my office, where I spent the majority of my time at my computer, printers, or files. A filthy table I'd found on the street held my workstation. To the right was the bar, about three feet tall, and equipped with bookshelves on the office side. Past that was the kitchen, same size as the office, with a small but fully functional gas range and oven, cooking gas being one of the many reasons I liked living far from the U.S. centers of commerce. I had a refrigerator, a coffee maker, a toaster oven, and a blender; I owned a mortar and pestle, an egg separator, and the other conveniences necessary to take food preparation seriously. Every counter, cabinet, and wall in my kitchen was splattered with grease and sauce stains, and a great deal of carbonized food remained stuck to the stovetop; I was proud of this ground-in filth, proud of the fact that I took food so much more seriously than cleanliness.

The bathroom was set off from the kitchen, and I did clean it occasionally, since my cat's box was in there, and since it's unethical and unwise to flush the toilet after each urination when living in the desert. The bathroom also contained the apartment's best feature: a large clawfoot tub next to a massive window overlooking Juarez. I am too tall to rest comfortably in a standard-sized tub, but I would sit in this tub almost every day, armed with a mixed drink and a book, letting the water and the border clothe me as best they could.

The bathroom also had a mirror, though it was not where I

first failed to recognize my face. A man can take care of his face for a long time without examining it. My hair was very short at the time, and required no comb. I "shaved" about once every four days; I would use an electric beard trimmer without a comb, resulting in very short stubble. Before going out, I would check my eyes for redness, and put drops in them as necessary. During this period, I doubt I could have told you their color.

I first realized what had happened in my bedroom, an open area vaguely separated from the office and kitchen by a few feet of wall and a wide, empty doorway. My bedroom was half the apartment; the size of the office and kitchen combined. The bedroom was exquisitely furnished by my landlord, who provided a dresser, a nightstand, and a very comfortable four-poster bed. There was also a tall vanity with a custom mirror atop it, measuring about three feet high and two feet wide. I had pushed the vanity and mirror to the foot of my bed, partly because they neatly took up the full length of the room and I didn't need the drawers in the vanity, so it was nice to have it, but have it out of the way, and partly because I had a vague idea that I'd like to watch myself fuck, though I never looked at the mirror while fucking. One morning, upon waking, I took my glasses from the nightstand and sat up in bed, rather than my usual habit of stumbling out of bed for a piss, then going back for my glasses. It was there, sitting up in bed, that I found I felt no connection to the face looking out at me from the vanity's mirror.

Alarmed, I looked away, then looked back, and away again. I crawled over to the mirror for a close look; the mirror was horrifically dirty, and I distracted myself with that momentarily, then jumped out of bed and rushed to the bathroom mirror, where close inspection revealed nothing. I had a carbuncle on my left cheekbone, and I knew it to be the same size as when I last examined it, but I did not recognize the shape of my cheekbones themselves. I recognized my haircut and the approximate length of my beard from last night, but both my chin and my forehead seemed alien. I realized that the expression on my face was one of shock, but it did not resemble my memories of seeing my own shocked face. I tried smiling, but saw that a forced smile could not be used to recognize a face under such circumstances. I went into the kitchen and poured and drank a shot, then touched the saltshaker a few times as I thought about that step in the tequila-drinking ritual. I returned to the mirror and studied my face for a long time, touching each feature in turn. I didn't come to any revelations, and when my shock finally faded, I tried out various expressions. I could not recognize my smiles or angry frowns — I recognized them as smiles and angry frowns, but I could not read the emotion behind them, and would not have known what to think if someone else flashed such expressions at me. I attempted other expressions, and found them forced.

I still recognized my eyebrows. When I arched them, they came up to a point. I liked that.

I spent a couple of days inside, alone, contemplating this change. Eventually, it was necessary to go out and check my Post Office box. Being in public was distressing; if any social encounters, positive or negative, transpired I would not know how my face appeared to others. I went out minimally; I had a lunch date that week, which I canceled. I checked my face constantly for familiar signs. None appeared.

This was not my first time living in that apartment. Between 2003 and 2008, I had five addresses in El Paso and perhaps a dozen addresses in different cities. At one point, I was staying in the house of a schizoaffective chain-smoker and searching for other lodging when another poet living in El Paso referred me to Sherman. I had met Sherman when he was managing one of his other properties, and he told me he had no space available — his various apartment properties were full, and the garret next to his house required a recommendation. With the other poet vouching for me, I was able to rent the garret, and stayed there for a very happy year before moving to Ohio and attempting a national poetry tour by hearse. The tour never got off the ground, and many addresses later, I found myself evicted and heartbroken in El Paso. I called Sherman, and he asked me to move back into my old place.

Moving back in was disorienting. It's a bit foolish for an adult to say, given a gap of a few years' time, "I was a different person then;" most of us change slowly, if at all. But one does often *feel* like a different person in the space of a few years. Thc carpet in the apartment was new (perhaps causing my apparent subconscious hostility towards it), and there was a new ceiling fan unit, but Sherman's quality furniture was all the same, and the bathroom, with its claw-foot tub that had housed so many drunk-and-stoned fucks, hadn't changed at all. My cat immediately recognized the garret, and treated our return as a homecoming; she was clearly thrilled to see I had been kicked out of my previous home, a house which included several other pets. I returned to the garret feeling directionless and outraged, with perfectly satisfied little housemate.

Still, it was a lovely apartment, and I did love the way I laid out the furniture. In the months building up to my identity confusion, I would spend many daytime hours, the shades drawn but the bedroom brightly illuminated by the desert summer, naked on the bed, watching myself in the vanity mirror. My chest was not particularly broad, and although my paunch was basically invisible while I was on my back, I knew it was there and did not forget it. But my body was mine, and the sight of it brought me great pleasure. The slight tanning that seeped in through my clothing seemed the perfect skin tone, and the thick, black, curly hair that covered my body never failed to strike me as beautiful. I would run my hands across it, starting with my armpits, across my nipples, where the hair was thickest, and to the center of my chest. I'd follow the narrow trail of hair to my stomach, where it spread over two-thirds of my width. Now erect, I would prop my legs up on the footboard, admiring the way my stomach, leg, and pubic hair formed one integrated coat, thicker in some places, but a consistent, holistic spread over my anterior. Delighting in my frame's length, I would hold my long, thin prick in one hand and a camera in the other. The mirror was at such an angle that I could see most of my body in it, from my knees to my shoulders, and never my face. I'd watch myself masturbate, trying to photograph the moment of orgasm, and often succeeding; always carefully photographing the come afterwards, be it pooled in my belly or splattered across my chest.

The tequila I drank was Viuda de Romero reposado, which sold for 96 pesos per liter at any convenience store in Juarez. Typically, I would combine the purchase of a bottle with other errands; I'd walk a mile south to downtown El Paso, run errands there, then walk another half-mile into Mexico. I would cross the Santa Fe International Bridge, paying 50 cents to enter Mexico. I'd walk two blocks down Avenida de Juarez to a corner shop called Del Rio, pay with a ten-dollar bill, and get either pesos or quarters in change. I'd walk two blocks back north and pay three pesos to cross the bridge again. Coming back into the country, I'd have to go through U.S. Immigration. There would be a long line to get into the U.S., and a much shorter line for U.S. Citizens. At the end of the line, I'd approach a Border Patrolman, who'd take my passport and ask me the reason for my visit. I'd present my liter of tequila, and tell him that I knew where to pay the tax. If I had been female, I would then have to answer several more questions about where I purchased the tequila and why, because El Paso Border Patrolmen did not know the difference between interrogation and flirting. Since I was male, I would move quickly through the process, allowing my backpack to be x-rayed, and paying the Texas Liquor Commission $1.25 for the import of the tequila. I would walk home, and usually drink the tequila with salt, though I was too lazy to stock limes.

When I had money and free time, I would combine the purchase of a bottle with an evening at the Kentucky Club. The first time I entered Juarez, I avoided the Kentucky Club since it was so clearly the place where white people went, but when I was finally dragged there by friends, the perfection of the place became obvious. The brass-accented interior is distinctly New Orleanian in flavor, and the sturdy mahogany bar, some fifty feet long, is neither properly polished or repaired. It is clearly an old bar, and clearly a *used* bar; the Francophilic decor offers an authentic cowboy-bar feel in a way that no place in El Paso ever could. Stories abound of the celebrities who've gotten plastered there; Marilyn Monroe is said to have celebrated her divorce from Arthur Miller at the Kentucky Club. It's allegedly the birthplace of the margarita, and while I admit some skepticism in that regard, doubt hardly matters when faced with the incredible taste and genuine strength of their 30-peso margaritas, by far the best I've ever tasted.

The Kentucky Club does attract tourists, and we Americans who continued to drink in Juarez after it erupted into open warfare tended to restrict ourselves to this bar. It also attracts its regular Juarense barflies, young couples on dates, and tipsy, flashily-dressed women who like to mock gringos, a game I'm always up for.

It was a couple of months after my crisis of identity that I looked in the mirror behind the Juarez bar and recognized myself. I was three margaritas in, which is to say five American margaritas in. I saw myself in the miror, a goofy gringo, laughing at his own arrogance and vanity, in an easy smile. I openly stared at myself for a moment, then looked away in embarrassment, but found myself constantly casting glances at the mirror that were probably not nearly as surreptitious as I'd like. I found myself making faces, practicing expressions like a 50s schoolgirl, and I recognized them; the ability to recognize my own emotions brought out sincere, and wonderfully familiar, tears.

I got very drunk that night, and stayed at the Hotel Juarez rather than walking home. When I woke up, I splashed water on my face, armpits, and crotch, and immediately returned to the Kentucky Club to examine myself. Once there, the reality hit me. I did not recognize myself because I was in the Kentucky Club, or because I was in Juarez. I recognized myself because the mirror there had an obvious brass finish; I looked familiar with a yellow patina.

Jonathan Penton is the editor and publisher of Unlikely Books. He is the author of three poetry books: *Last Chap, Blood and Salsa*, and *Painting Rust.*

Andrew Gallix

Dr. Martens' Bouncing Souls

It didn't hit me at first. Not straight away it didn't. For a few long seconds there, the world was freeze-framed. I half expected to see tumbleweed blow by. All around, people emitted muffled sounds as if sporting ball-gags under water. Possibly swathed in cotton wool, they spoke in slow motion, their syllables hideously elongated like limbs on the rack. I distinctly recall being put in mind of an unravelling audio cassette, or one of those avant-garde sound poems that were all the rage back in the day. And then it hit me.

Hard.

Really hard.

Repeatedly.

To describe the pain as excruciating just wouldn't do it justice. It was unspeakable, unsputterable; not even stutterable — utterly unutterable. What I *can* attempt to convey, however — to a certain degree, at least, though not, alas, to the third — is the unrelenting nature of the whole episode. I was stunned. Dumbfounded. Gobsmacked. At a loss for words. Mouth agog, screaming on mute. Bent triple, pissing bleeding blood. Pummelled into that liminal zone beyond which no representation is possible. With the benefit of hindsight, I see it as a crash course in transgression, no less. Nothing would ever be the same again. Not quite. Not for me. Uh-uh. Blown was my mind. Rocked were my foundations. Shaken was my core. Topsy-turvy was my world. Over tit was my arse. And then it hit me again.

Hard.

Really hard.

Really, really hard.

Repeatedly.

Repeatedly.

Repeatedly.

Repeatedly . . .

I blame it on Effie. Effing Effie and her fucking iffy frock. A brown flower-print number, the kind usually modelled by ladies of a certain age. Ladies who have long ceased to turn heads. Ladies who are fading away inexorably. Ladies who are almost invisible already. Ladies who, even as we speak, are being cut out of the equation with tiny toenail scissors. Slowly. Surely. Snip, snip — snip. But draped around Effie's nubility it became impossibly erotic, as if the breath of life had suddenly been pumped into a long deflated blow-up doll. As if all the old biddies in their flower-print dresses were in bloom again, having magically recovered their pertness of yore. As if our very planet were a tight pair of bouncy buttocks and the whole wide universe had a massive hard-on.

Hard.

Really hard.

Rock-hard.

Rock on.

Blowing mellow bellows from below, a cheeky breeze sported with the hem. Effie even had to hold it down on occasion, which lent her an air of charming vulnerability. Despite this precaution, and after a great deal of hemming and hawing, the flimsy material finally resolved to flare up, possibly in answer to the prayers of all those who had slowed down to admire the young lady's graceful sway. Time almost came to a standstill as the dress made its giddy ascent in the manner of a Big Dipper inching up the steepest of Battersea slopes. I half expected to see tumbleweed blow by. Then suddenly — amid a cacophony of catcalls, wolf whistles and screeching tyres — the world went into overdrive frock'n'roll-style. Effie gasped in surprise, looking back instinctively to see how many oglers would be going home with a spring in their proverbial and diaphanous black lace on their minds. As she did so, I couldn't help but notice the imaginary ejaculates from a hundred passers-by glistening in her hair like so many constellations of icicles. It was hard not to really.

Really hard.

Really, really hard.

The heat was well and truly on. You could almost feel the sap rising as Effie walked by. Men for miles around seemed to be picking up illicit frequencies, pricking up their ears at the mere sound of her killer heels in the distance. I tried to throw them off the scent by accelerating or crossing the road at regular intervals, but to no avail. I knew I would bump into him eventually, or rather he would bump into me. He was out there somewhere — everywhere — whoever he may be. It was just a matter of time now, and now was the time. He loomed up, he loomed large, hurtling towards me with all the inevitability of tragedy. There was no way I could avoid him. In fact, he veered slightly to the right to ensure that we were on a collision course. It was fight or flight. It was lose face and face loss. It was too fucking late.

Effie didn't notice anything at first. She pursued her monologue looking straight ahead as he rammed into me, only pulling up when I remonstrated with my assailant. This, of course, was the cue he had been waiting for. I was playing right into his big lumberjack hands, which he balled into mighty fists before felling me like a sapling. Effie screamed while I attempted to regain verticality by means of the wall. Paying no heed to the abuse that was being hurled his way, he slowly removed his jacket and folded it rather fastidiously. By the time he had finished rolling up his shirtsleeves, Effie had run out of expletives or patience. I noticed how she rolled her eyes in desperation as I finally staggered to my feet, still puffing and panting, only to hear that I was going to be taught a bloody good lesson in front of my wife. And then he hit me again. Hard. Really hard. Repeatedly. He decked me, then he floored me, then he pulled me up again and decked me some more. At first I was under the cosh, but I soon became conversant with the sentence that was being executed with such surgical precision; I could even distinguish the nuances of each blow. It was like learning a new language.

Taking on the demeanour of an impartial spectator at a boxing match, Effie stepped back to embrace the whole scene. She was more open-minded now, wanted to hear him out. She was hedging her bets: let the best man win, like. At one point — a couple of cheeky jabs followed by a cracking right cross — she even started seeing his, which he put across so eloquently, so forcefully. After all, he was only being fair. Firm but fair. So fair and so firm. Hard, really hard. With her arms folded across her ample bosom, she looked down upon me, sighing and shaking her head, as if she thought, on reflection, that a good lesson would indeed do me the world of good.

She was bowing to the inevitable, submitting to a superior force and was silently urging me to do likewise, to let go. All resistance was futile: I had this coming all along and now it had come, and that was that. It was in the order of things to put things in order. It felt right; it even felt good, so good. Hard, so hard. The wicked gleam in her eye proved that she was now baying for blood. Baying, obeying some primitive urge. Harder, really harder.

After an uppercut and a left hook had left me on my knees again, begging for mercy, he slipped his jacket back on and bitch-slapped me to the ground. Blinking through the streaming blood, I caught a glimpse of my wife's expensive black panties as she stepped over me to join him. They walked away hand in hand.

Andrew Gallix lives in Paris where he teaches at the Sorbonne University and edits *3:AM Magazine*. He is writing a book about unwritten books. More at www.andrewgallix.com.

Pig Bodine

Pig Bodine Solves the US Immigration and Education Dilemmas in One Blow

The beauty of these two US problems, immigration and education, is their clear solution, a true no-brainer that kills two birds with one stone.

The immigration dilemma regards the influx of Hispanics and is spurred by racist hysteria and fear that jobs will be lost. The latter fear is a response to an underlying reality: most of the jobs held in the US by those white folks born in the US are nothing more than middle class welfare, make-work granted as part of the privilege of being a white person born in the US. The fear is that the US economy will eventually need to produce something to export besides Treasury Bills in case foreign money stops supporting the massive white middle class welfare program.

The second problem is related to the first. The fact is, US high school students graduate with the equivalent of a grade school European or Asian education, a lower middle school Latin American education. Not only are the graduates unable to do arithmetic, let along mathematics, they cannot reason, think abstractly or even read with comprehension. Most of them can recognize a nominal list of English words and understand short sentences composed of uncomplicated combinations of those words, but few of them can assemble one of these strings with semantic content using the rules of grammar, and fewer yet are able to understand this sentence. The same is true of US college graduates. It seems only thirty percent of them can read with comprehension; further breakdown of that figure indicates a significant portion of those who graduate from US colleges and who can read are foreign born.

The education crisis ostensibly regards mathematics. The problem seems to be that almost no one in the US can do mathematics,a discipline that politicians and journalists endlessly confuse with arithmetic. This is likely because said politicians and journalists are unable to do anything so abstract as to add fractions, let along set up and solve an algebra problem based on a written description (the dreaded "word" problem, not to confused with the word problem for groups).

The President of the US has appointed an administrator from the University of Texas to head up a commission on the mathematics problem, Larry Faulkner. Consider what Faulkner said:

"The object is to find the best path for getting kids prepared to go into algebra and to succeed in algebra. That course is a gate-keeping course in so many ways."

Excuse me, but algebra in the sense used here, meaning to solve simple equations containing unknowns by using memorized algorithms, is the intellectual equivalent of learning to add and multiply. These may be difficult tasks for Faulkner, who at one time happened to be a chemistry professor, not a subject known for its application of abstract mathematics, but they are not mathematics. To call algebra gate-keeping is akin to saying the crux of literature is spelling. The gate-keeping courses are four semesters of calculus through solving a certain class of ordinary differential equations and extensions to higher dimensions. Mathematics begins with these, branching directly into analysis and also into algebra as the study of groups, rings, vector spaces, modules, and other fundamental structures. Algebra as Faulkner means it is arithmetic with symbols, and is essentially on the level of abstraction required of grade school.

The solution: Give a national exam on the level of Japanese or European middle school mathematics, that is through ordinary differential equations and multivariate calculus, to all US high school and college graduates and if they fail to make a minimal score or get a professional sports contract, strip them of their citizenship and deport them, bringing in an equal number of real workers to replace them. It could be people willing to pick crops or cut meat or clean motels or to work in aerospace engineering or computer engineering. Language would be a small problem since those being deported are not likely to ever master English anyway, having been given the chance of a lifetime and failed.

There are minor problems, the most obvious being the US Constitution which gives anyone born in the US citizenship, but it is certain that the Supreme Court's Strict Constructionists will find a way use the founding father's documented bigotry and love of cheap labor to get around this amendment. More difficult may be finding a country to take the useless, lazy US high school and college grads, but certainly some country can be found to accept them for a nominal fee. Perhaps Somalia. It would be worth the cost to be rid of bozos with high expectations of entitlement to nonproductive, even counterproductive jobs among the class of highly paid non-contributing social parasites in some sort of upper middle class welfare position like management, law, government, medicine, finance, or sales. This would in turn help relieve the problem of needing so many foreign graduate students in mathematics to teach the remedial courses required by US high school graduates, noting that any mathematics through the four semesters of elementary calculus is remedial. Anyone graduating from high school ought to know as much mathematics, as is the case in the rest of the developed world.

Likely it would be best to begin the program with those teaching in the public schools, replacing deported teachers with people educated in academic disciplines instead of ceremonially certified by a teaching bureaucracy insuring the incompetent take to the classrooms. After all, a good deal of US remedial college course work is to undo the nonsense implanted during high school and below.

This could also model a program to ease another educational problem, namely that US high school graduates are not only semiliterate in their native tongue, but can't speak any other languages either. Instead of forcing them to take pesky courses in French, Spanish, German or British English, why not extend the law making US English the official language of the US to the entire world? The US military could be built up to enforce US English as the official world language. All works of literature in other languages would be expunged, anyone not learning English exiled to the Moon and later to Mars, and history modified in accord with current US educational policies to no longer mention there ever were such aberrant tongues.

Of course there is the problem of enforcing the usage of US English. A model program could begin within the US with a Language Police to enforce the English only law. Special courts could be given authority to put those who make grammatical mistakes in re-education camps for a year. If after the year those interned are unable to pass the TOEFL, they would be exiled. Of course, the US would likely end up exiling President Bush, but then they would also exile most of the network news anchors and commentators as well.

Especially egregious would be the offense of omitting *-ly* from the end of adverbs formed from adjectives. The law might also include a "cliche clause" to punish the overuse of words like impact, particularly hybrid usages which are now so popular among the quasi-literate. Random quizzes on correct usage of lay and lie, for example, or affect and effect, as well to, too and two, among other words, would be in order.

It seems reasonable to begin the use of the Language Police within Congress, as they are the ones passing the official English law, and begin deporting those who abuse the language within that august body. After Congress is cleansed of those who do not know US English, the police could move on the country at large, perhaps beginning with the suburbs of DC.

There exists another potential solution. The US wants to become a nation of managers, and since one cannot be a manager without workers to manage, control the borders and allow in ten workers for every US citizen who makes it to twenty-five years of age. Amend the constitution to give all those born in the US an MBA at age twenty-five, together with their ten workers, and a token annual salary of $100,000, adjusted for inflation. This obviates the need for education, since the end goal of US education, a ceremonial certificate, is already accomplished. The age restriction ensures people are kept off the job market, thus fulfilling the other purpose of US schools. Those weirdoes who want to learn something can go to other countries to accomplish this. For border control, build a fence containing the entire lower forty-eight states. Make it a mile wide and 200 feet tall and dot it with sensors. Raising the money for all this is not a problem. Perform the modern equivalent of printing money: have the US Treasury sell bonds to the public and then have the US Federal Reserve System buy those bonds, building up the supply of high-powered money. Trivial.

Sample exam questions are available on request, but the key is not to make the exam available to schools in advance. The exam should be made up from a syllabus through calculus texts like Lang and Apostol. Those who write the exam should not be actively involved in teaching in public schools, to avoid the potential hazard of teaching to the test as is currently done in most US schools.

Study Cites Lack of Talent

Someone hands me a newspaper folded to a headline proclaiming that "lack of talent in the US feeds offshoring". I'm prepared to read about how the US will soon produce its television programs in Mumbai, or how we're going to scour China for candidates for next American Idol, the current crop so talentless even rockers notice. But no; the article, admittedly written by a journalist, is so confused it becomes what it attempts to tell. Is there a word for this, like onomatopoeia, for such a hapless misunderstanding that it becomes what it purports to report? A Latin expression for an article imitating the very problem it intends denuding?

Granted, journalists tend not to learn much of anything except how to pen leaden prose necessary to convince readers they bear heavy messages. Moreover, I have not read the report, The Globalization of White-Collar Work, that Jonathan B. Cox purports to illumine in his article, though experience reading newspaper articles regarding economics (I have been told the same is true of science, mathematics and engineering) has taught me journalists never get anything right. If a mistake is possible, it will be made; if not, a way will be invented.

The upshot of the article seems to be that this report claims jobs move offshore not only to save money, but also because talent is not available in the US. I don't understand what is meant here. There is likely a massive pool of talent in the US. What seems missing is a certain set of skills. In our rush to provide each and every breathing US citizen a college degree, we have dropped the purported goal of schooling, namely education; that is to say, the ability to read and to think. Granted far fewer are awarded degrees in this faraway place "offshore," but when they are it tends to mean they actually learned something. For the most part in our make-work economy here in the US, where nothing is demanded besides pieces of paper certifying the right class, skills are unnecessary. But to maintain such an economy in a global setting is difficult to impossible.

And consider the chimp elected as President of the US, likely part of that 30% of college grads from his generation unable to read with comprehension anything beyond newspapers. (The number for the current generation is 70%; that is to say, 70% of college grads in this generation are unable to read with comprehension.) If a semi-literate bozo who eschews reading can become President of the United States, why would anyone bother to read or to think? (Of course, not many have his father's friends.) Though it needs to be remembered that the voters recently bitch-slapped the man and his brain, Karl Rove, into some semblance of reality for starting a pointless war they could not win on the cheap. Perhaps some booklarning might have saved them from such a gross error.

But the article talks about talent. That makes no sense. Talent is not needed. The desire to work and, God forbid, to think are what is needed. The fundamental ability to read and to reason. And granted some missing specific skills. This is the second confusion in the article.

It says, and I quote:

"Too few students are getting advanced degrees in science and math, and companies can't import enough foreign workers because of visa limitations."

This is contrary to every study I have seen. Advanced degrees in science and mathematics do not get jobs, certainly not high paying jobs. MBAs get high paying jobs, lawyers get high paying jobs, physicians get high paying jobs, and even engineers can get high paying jobs from time to time. Not scientists or mathematicians. So where does this bit of nonsense come from?

Here is the confusion in a nutshell:

"Companies worldwide are scouring the globe for the best programmers, engineers and other professionals."

That may be true. I know plenty of people from around the world with degrees in computer science and other forms of engineering who are able to get jobs, though their opportunities in the US are limited. (Many US companies have told their software engineers to find other ways to contribute or ship out, other ways meaning either management or marketing.) For the most part, US students are too lazy and ill-prepared to study mathematics, science or engineering. They all want to become instantaneously rich and famous as broadcast journalists or business moguls, though none of the business moguls I know about ever studied bidness (and most never graduated from college).

The confusion is this: Science and mathematics are not engineering, and they have little to do with one another. There are certain forms of computational facility required for certain types of engineers, with the most abstract needed by electrical and control engineers, sometimes by mechanical engineers. But at most this amounts to a formulaic approach to differential equations, linear algebra, a modicum of probability, a minor acquaintance with the Fourier transform. Nothing outside low-level undergraduate courses, certainly not the stuff of advanced degrees. Sometimes a little physics helps, but not on a formal level. I have known oodles of excellent computer programmers (or as they prefer to be called, software engineers) who know far less mathematics than I. In fact, software engineering requires next to no mathematics at all.

So why such an inane confusion, akin to confusing the practice of medicine, a form of engineering, with the doing of science? Perhaps it goes back to the journalist, unless the study itself is badly flawed. More likely it is a combination, since one of the authors of the study, Arie Lewin, seems to be an academic practitioner of business and sociology, two areas devoid of science and mathematics and reason.

It may also go back to the hogwash fed US youngsters by their formerly doped-up parents, now foolish grandparents, telling their spawn how creative and gifted they were. And these dupes believed it and acted as if it were true, and passed it on to their even lazier, more aggressively coddled spawn.

Nonetheless, it is telling as to why the US is so backward, since the highly educated who are writing these reports don't know shit from Shinola. (™)

Suffice it to say that the talented, the creative, gifted people in science and mathematics are worthless as tits on a boar. Just as the musically talented have no chance of making it with a musical career unless they quash or hide that talent. Aesthetically handicapped, brain-bound crazies.

Let's face it. The US is now officially lazy-land, with an educational system borrowed from Texas, soon able to proudly display the very bumper sticker now only displayed in Texas, Stupid and Proud of It. I wonder if that has been patented as a business process.

Pig Bodine, M.Sc., Ph.D., BM2, BEM, MAD, MDMA, descends from a long line of able-bodied seamen, his ancestors having served first in the Royal Navy and then in the US Navy during and after the Revolutionary War. It is rumored that they served with Viking invaders of Britain before settling near the coast, boatswain's mates all. Pig is the first member of his clan to obtain a meaningless ceremonial certificate in a prestigious area of bullshit. Inspired by the inflated egos of the likes of the useless Dick Armey and Phil Gramm, after his 30 years in the US Navy, Pig obtained a doctorate in economics at a third-rate state university and taught for a time at a fifth-rate shit university in Texas. Unlike those two role models, he did not work the corporate gloryholes of the beltway.

Pig is an author, speaker and knot tier. In fact, his expertise in tying knots is acknowledged world wide. He has won knot tying contests in almost every nation on earth. He began his academic career studying knot theory but realized it was far too useful a discipline and so switched to economics, a study with no known applications to the real world. He later conceded that as useless as economics is, it would have been better to study business administration, a far more useless and dangerous academic program but he had lost interest in being a useless turd. Pig likes to say, "Nobody with a bullshit degree in economics needs to be justified."

Deb Hoag

Midnight with Turtle

He's scrawny as hell, but with thick ridges of muscle across his belly and his ribs. Knotted ropes of muscle on his arms and shoulders. I know this because, as disdainful as he is of mundane hygiene, he takes his shirt off every chance he gets to parade his youth and beauty around in front of all the less blessed.

Hair is blonde and messy, greasy at the roots and electric at the tips, catching the sunlight and looking like it could float right off his head if it weren't rooted to his scalp. His eyes are derisive, whenever they make contact, which is infrequently. I was introduced to him on a Tuesday, and his glance barely skittered over me before I was dismissed. His unwillingness to make even bare bones social noises was a little disconcerting, but not my problem. Oh well.

He's at my best friend Narleen's house because he's *sofa surfing*. That means he's been kicked out of every other home that's been opened to him, and his aunt's couch is his last resort.

I got involved because Nar and her husband are going on a cruise, and she doesn't trust him to water the plants, much less feed the cat and change the litter. Nar's one of my best friends. She always says exactly what she thinks without being mean, a quality I greatly admire. I want to be just like her when I grow up, and in the meantime, I hang around, hoping some of that skill will become mine by osmosis.

I listen as Nar tries to explain to me how Turtle ended up camped in her living room. "He's . . . I don't know what he is. I don't think he's all there, sometimes. I used to think he was the kid most likely to. Now? Something happened to him. Drugs, maybe. Everybody else has given him the boot. He won't work, won't help out, and acts like he's doing you a favor by being there."

I raise and eyebrow and she laughs. "That's what they say, anyway. He's been okay here, so far. Still, I don't want to take chance of something happening while I'm gone."

Briefly, I contemplate what I would do if *something happened* while Nar was gone. Call 911? Man the fire extinguishers? Throw a life preserver? Take him down in hand-to-hand? Assuming that the *something* happened during the fifteen minutes a day I planned on being there.

"I don't think he would hurt her or anything," she goes on, referring to the cat. "Not like I'd come home and find Sweetpea disemboweled in the living room, with odes to Satan written on my walls in her blood — but I could see him forgetting her food and water and then sneering about how bourgeois it is to have a house pet, like he did me a favor by starving her half to death. You know what I mean?"

Totally. I totally know what she means. An anti-social, narcissistic asshole, who doesn't mind shifting the blame for his own lack of responsibility on anyone who happens to be handy. Harsh, I know, but I'm off the clock. It means I get to have opinions like everybody else.

That's before I walk in the house on Saturday morning and see him up close. He looks like he forgot I was coming, looks like he forgot who I was. Maybe he's forgotten who he is. Totally possible from the terrified look in his eye. He looks like he hasn't slept in days. Or nights. Not good. Either that he can't track who I am from last Tuesday, or that he can't figure out what to do about a middle-aged woman with a key entering his aunt's house at 9 am on a Saturday morning.

"Hey, Turtle," I say, easing in the door. His eyes flick here, there, settle on a spot on the ceiling as if the Ten Commandments are written there. One of his hands is jittering against his thigh. The cat comes out and winds around my feet, probably relieved as hell to see someone who's not looking for answers to their problems on the roof. "Remember me? Your aunt Nar asked if I'd stop in and feed Sweetpea."

We both look down at the furball currently making love to my ankles. In an abrupt change of attitude, Turtle sneers and mutters something I can't quite catch, then makes an ironically sweeping, gallant gesture to invite me the rest of the way in. As soon as the door closes, he retreats to the computer, where a smoldering pie plate bears witness that his aunt's rule about no smoking in the house has already been violated.

Fortunately for both of us. I'm not the cigarette police. Nar can deal with it when she gets back. Turtle could be in an Internet-induced coma for all the awareness he shows for the rest of my visit, except for the feet tapping madly on the floor and the cigarettes he burns through relentlessly. I feed the cat, check on the litterbox, which looks like it can go a few more days. Actually, as far as I'm concerned, it can probably go all week, with a quick change just before the cruisers get back. Who's going to tell, the cat? I'm already pretty sure it won't be Turtle.

I get ready to leave and pause by the door. "It was nice to see you again, Turtle. You doing okay here? You need anything?"

Again with the flickering eyes. What is that I see scurrying around in there behind that gorgeous hazel? He looks like he wants to speak, then shakes his head. "I'm good," he says, and turns back to the computer. He cocks his head as if listening to something I can't hear.

"Okay, bye. See you tomorrow. About the same time, I guess." No response. I close the door and leave.

When I get home, I shoot Nar an email, just in case she's hooked up. "Everything fine at home. Kid and cat still alive. House in one piece." I don't mention the smoking. "I'll keep you posted."

The next morning, on my way, I remember the confusion, the fear, the thing he wanted to say and didn't. I pick up a pack of Marlboros and some donuts. And milk. Kids like milk. Even grown kids.

"Hey, Turtle, I'm here," I call as I come in the door, feeling stupid balancing keys/purse/donuts/milk.

No kid, no cat. What the fuck? I make my way through the house, and find him in his aunt's bed, pie plate full of cigarette butts on the nightstand, cat sleeping on his ass. I back out, leave the donuts and smokes on the counter, put the milk in the fridge. I check the cat's food and water. All good. I go to work.

The next day. Turtle's on the computer. "Hey, I came by yesterday but you were asleep. Did you get the donuts?"

We both look at the counter. The box has disappeared. He mutters something in a contemptuous voice. I pick out the words "refined sugar", but spot the box in the trash, and the little cellophane window shows the donuts are all gone.

"You're welcome," I reply.

"You left those?" It's the first time he's actually spoken to me other than to mutter some caustic remark as a reply to a direct question. I wonder who else he thought might have left them. The donut fairy?

His eyes focus on a spot to his left, and he tilts his head. Listening to something I can't hear again. Dollars to donuts, he's psychotic. Responding to internal stimuli, as we say in the biz. Or stoned. Hard to tell as little as we've interacted.

"Hey, Turtle," I say, gently, before he gets too far gone.

Reluctantly, he tears his eyes away from whatever they were focused on and gives me a flicker of attention. His eyes run away like my face is melting and he's trying to pretend he doesn't notice.

"What do you want for breakfast tomorrow?"

The eyes track back. He thinks. "Donuts were good."

"Coffee?"

It's almost a smile. "No sugar." Sugar's okay in donuts, but not in coffee. Got it. The kind of contradiction I totally understand.

When I get home, I shoot Nar an email. "Cat still alive. You should have warned me the kid was such a chatterbox. Talk to you later."

The next morning, I come bearing donuts and coffee. And more Marlboros. What the hell am I doing?

He's nowhere to be seen, and I make noise in the kitchen, call his name. He appears out of the bedroom door, blinking and startled, and I feel a pang of guilt. He looks panicked, but I offer him caffeine and sugar and he settles quick enough.

"Your aunt says you're looking for work." That merits a sneer. He mumbles something in which I catch the word 'whoring'. I'm thinking he's referring to the idea of working for a living, not his aunt, and proceed on that assumption. "What kind of work do you do?"

He shakes his head, looks to the left. No answer. "Maybe I should ask you what you want to do. What do you like doing?"

"Light shows."

That he has an answer at all comes as quite a surprise. He

seems like such a lump. The muscles tell me he does more than walk from couch to computer during the day, but I've never *seen* him be anything but passive. He puts something out there, too? I proceed with caution, trying to figure out how not to sound like a total moron, as he waits for me to say something back.

"Light shows like . . . for bands?" I hazard, thinking Pink Floyd and stadium lasers and earning the sneer.

"Light shows like . . . performance art." I must still look confused. "In the dark. With strobes." I am confused. He sounds like he's speaking to a child, enunciating every word with care. I wonder if there's a planet, or a basement, where he makes sense.

"I've never seen anything like that before," I venture, finally, still having no idea what he's talking about. "Would you show me sometime?"

"Sure," he responds immediately, then tilts his head. "Well, maybe." He listens some more. "Probably not. I'm not an . . . entertainer for people." With each word, his speech gets thicker, slower, quieter, until he's mumbling again. It's like that voice in his head rides a big wave of mud that descends and sludges him into submission. I actually think I can see it coming and going in his eyes, his face. Like those lenses they click in front of your eyes at the optometrist's. Clear/cloudy clear/cloudy clear/cloudy. I wonder if he sees the irony in wanting to do shows without showing anyone. I feel a wave of pity.

"In the dark . . . like at night?"

He nods and chooses another donut with great care.

I don't know why I'm pressing; it's no skin off my nose, either way. But it's intriguing, and I love people puzzles. It's why I do what I do. "If I came by tonight, could you show me?"

He mutters, but his head is going up and down, so I act like I got a yes. "Cool," I say, before he can object. "I'll bring dinner. See you tonight." And I'm off into the wild world of mental health, wondering what I'll see tonight.

Before I leave work, I send an email to Nar. "Turtle's doing a light show tonight. Everything's good. Talk to you tomorrow." On the way back, I pick up Chinese.

We sit at the table and eat mu shu pork. Turtle's wearing

black: black jeans, black tee, black hoodie. He mutters about MSG, but digs in. Suddenly, his head comes up and he gives me a glare. "Look, do you want sex?"

I almost laugh, but pity wins. "Nope, Turtle. Just to see what you do. Light show now?"

He glances out the window. "In a few minutes. It needs to be all the way dark."

We go back to eating.

When we're done, Turtle pronounces it dark enough, and we shut off all the interior lights and go out onto the back porch, Turtle clutching a ragged cardboard box. He opens it, and takes out two fist-sized frosted plastic globes, which he holds by a short cord. I sit in one of the lawn chairs, and he bows to me, very formal, then moves to turn off the porch light.

There's no moon, but we're up in the White Mountains, and stars burst from the sky like living things. Maybe they are. The sudden absence of light is like a living thing, too, pulsing against my eyes, swimming up against my skin like cool water. Trees rustle, I hear vague sounds from the main road, and smell those layered summer scents: barbecue and watered lawns and a faint whiff of skunk that somebody's dog stirred up.

There's a click and music starts, not too loud, something funky and electronic, which should clash horribly with the rural backyard nighttime, but sounds okay anyways. Suddenly there is a rip in the dark, and colored lights — red, blue, green — strobe madly. Faint, behind them, I can see Turtle, standing still and focused. His head is up, hair covered by the black hood on his sweatshirt. I think his eyes are closed, as he stands, the colored balls of light balanced on his palms. For a second, I wonder if this is it — Turtle standing in the dark, still as a statue, while the lights flash off and on in his palms.

Then he starts to move.

He's slow at first, but there's grace — always grace. It looks like he's gliding through the poses of some ancient Chinese fighting form, the way they're always doing in Kung Fu movies. The crane, the crouching dog, the dancing lion. The lights keep flashing. He picks up speed, now moving like a boxer, hands flying, and the flashing of the lights begins to stream together, making colored ribbons in the air. He must be holding them by the cords now, because the lights are spinning, criss-crossing each other, and the music is revving up, and the damn kid never misses a beat.

He's a body genius.

We live in a society of the desk-bound, where thinking — linear, logical thinking — is prized above everything else. But there are other kinds of intelligence — kinesthetic intelligence, for example, coordination and control and brilliant movement, and this incoherent little guy has it in spades.

And endurance. The music goes on and on, pounding, ripping through the air. It seems louder now, and I can't hear anything else, but maybe that's just because I'm letting myself be sucked into Turtle-land. And still he goes, spinning the balls so fast that they turn into long, slinky tubes of light that spray out against the night like glittering snakes. I can smell his sweat now, sharper than the skunk. And still he goes.

Finally, the music stops, and so does Turtle. I jump to my feet. I clap. Its overwhelming, the beauty, the expressiveness that's come out of the flat-faced little son-of-a-gun, and I want him to know. He's fucking awesome. I can see his face in the light from the little strobes, now resting in his hands again like pets. His lungs are working like bellows. Sweat is streaming from his face, and he's smiling. He looks right at me.

"You liked it."

"You're a fricking wizard, Turtle! That was amazing!"

He does something and the little strobes wink off, and he throws himself in the lawn chair next to mine. I can hear him breathing as my eyes adjust. He flicks his cigarette lighter, and sets a citronella candle ablaze, then lights a cigarette. Together with his sweat, the smells aren't bad, some exotic Turtle incense.

I'm content to sit, think about what I saw, about the surprises people hold. After a few minutes, I ask a lazy question. "What kind of lights are those?"

"Poi. Poi lights."

The lights whisper of dark clubs, grinding bodies and loud music, Ecstasy. I wonder if that's how the Turtle-train got derailed.

Maybe I'll Google them later.

We talk for a while, desultory things, almost a normal conversation, although his thoughts get a little jumbled from time to time. Still, it's not that hard to follow his train of thought, and it's kind of fun, jumping from one subject to the next to the next. Poetry, wrestling, politics, skateboards. The conversation ebbs and flows, and eventually I check my watch. Getting late, nearly the witching hour. Time for me to be home in bed. *Sans* my best friend's crazy nephew.

"I hear things," he says, suddenly.

"I guessed."

"Sometimes I see things, too."

"Bad things?"

There's a movement, Turtle shrugging. If you shrug in the dark and no one can see, is it still an answer?

"I'm crazy. I'm not like normal people."

I do him the favor of not lying to him, not rushing in with a bunch of reassuring bullshit. I just nod and we sit in lawn chairs together. I think about what Nar told me, about how a few years ago, she thought, "he's the kid mostly likely to," and now he's sleeping on couches and thinking magical beings bring him donuts in the morning. The psychotic break breaks hard for some people.

"Crazy doesn't mean *over*. I could probably find somebody to help you with that. There's medicine that can shut down the voices. Mostly."

"I've heard about that," he says gravely. "But I'm afraid . . . part of me would go away with them. I'm just not sure. Sometimes, I just . . . bleed . . . a little, and they stop being bad. That's better than drugs."

I can see he's facing straight ahead, but his eyes are trying to come back to me, to see how I'm taking it.

"I know people who cut themselves to feel better. On their arms, on their legs, places people won't notice. Not to kill themselves, but just to feel a little better."

Without a word, he pulls up a pant leg and stretches his foot out in the light. Up and down his shin, silver scars criss-cross like fractal lace.

"Oh, Turtle." I breathe. "There's so much pain there."

He pulls back his leg, pushes his jeans back down.

"It's a high price to pay for peace."

"Will you make me do it?"

I shake my head. "No." The cuts are superficial, not life-threatening. Lots of people cut, more than a person who's never done crisis work would think. There are so many people who cut they have fucking Internet groups Pretty soon they're going to have a lobby. "It would be a good thing if you did, though. And you could always stop if you don't like how it feels. Will you think about it?"

He lights a cigarette. Even in the candlelight I can see the old nicotine stains on those young fingers. His life is more fragile than the flame, and its already slipping away from him.

"Will you bring donuts in the morning?"

"Yep."

"I'll think about it."

We say good night. "Turtle," I say as we walk back through the house. "People have all kinds of problems, all kinds of things happen to us. But we all have a turning point where we get to choose what we're going to do with the problems and the troubles. We still get to choose."

He shrugs and mutters something. I realize the mud in his brain is back, possibly worse because he actually managed to step out of it for a little while. One step forward, one step back.

I go home and email Nar: "Cat doing well, kid's surviving. Couch unscarred, house still stands. You didn't want any of that furniture anyway, did you? Kidding, I swear. Talk to you tomorrow."

It's two am and I fall asleep seeing snakes of brilliant light bursting against my lids. I wonder what it's like to hear voices so terrifying you cut yourself to make them go away, so beautiful you cut yourself rather than take pills that would get them out of your head forever. What do they whisper, shout, cry out? Only Turtle knows.

Deb Hoag has been writing professionally for going on 20 years, starting at a weekly alternative newspaper in Detroit , Michigan , The Metro Times. In the early '90s, Deb went back to school and was awarded a PhD in clinical psychology at the University of Detroit-Mercy. Since embarking on her new career, Deb's worked on the White Mountain Apache Indian Reservation in a variety of mental health positions, as in-patient therapist at the psychiatric hospital in Show Low, Arizona , and now lives and works in Flagstaff. You can find many of her short stories, in Polluto Magazine, where she's a regular contributor. Dog Horn Press published her novel *Crashin' the Real* in 2009. Her novel *Dr. Gonzo* is coming out at Burning Man, first week of September, from Unlikely Books. And a midgrade novel, *The Dragon's Secret,* is making its debut through Artix Entertainment in August of 2010. It's written by Lyra Solis, who looks a lot like Deb but without all the swearing and sexing.

Dave Migman

Learning How to Live and Die

Prologue

The West dissolves into the promise of its repose: blood feuds and orgies, a cross between convicts, sucking out juices, faeces, pus and semen, masticated and spewed back out to form the mortar of a new social contract soiled by snuff-terrorist-paedophiles. Under age girls and boys sticking it to each other, the *'new teen sex addicts'* fuck like rabbits between doses of adverts *'how to improve your sex appeal'* — dress less the elders're worthless media mogul conspirators bearing their allegiance on their palms. Transfer this logo to your flesh — the brand be good don't cross the line into radicalism, bearded anarchist madmen Bin Laden fascists Islamic moneylender lefty commie EN-EMY always (indelible, a brand name) THEMselves the empire of rats, the nation of a pampered, bored elite, cushion happy *oh god my hair disaster oh god bleach the flesh* white is still success *ah* this fickle reflection. The flicker morality, our lack of control in a society thus controlled by the veneer of the tome, saviours' politics and preachers back home to abuse the system in the system

the system above the law but lower
no!
. . . cities so fat on it they spew out their entrails into the country. Each one a virilant sore chewing on the Goddess cunt sticking out more lights to block out the moon's original glow, more toxins to choke more things to fill our bins more more so we stand in lines glaring at the checkout sow cursing queues, consumerism, plastic bags — but we're all in it, *fill them* it's easier that way, to fill the hate, to keep away. Disengage.

The Dream

night now, quiet now, between the humming computers, the breath of transference

data spiders stranded behind cupboards. tomorrow I climb into the beast, a silver tube into the blue. attica calling. away from all this . . .

i am getting the fuck out of here. i am leaving this all behind.

Day One

costa cafe gatwick 3am

"it's all up here." says the dopey girl with the 6ft wide head. It's all up there, "*look*", a list of brand names. "*good, let's go, let's proliferate.*" there she is, her giant billboard face, searching, soulless eyes cast over her shoulder, a cocaine hungry grin. but there is something else in her face, alongside the apparent docility, if you focus on the shadowed side, plain as day, the malice of want, the malice of brand names and the lust of trinkets.

(we came down into a void. where's the fucking ground? down into a gullet, like we might never land, like there was nothing. just an endless hole)

Day Two

a shape, wheeling thru the darkness. thin tyres on sand, sweeping round the bend. a bike, must be a local, knows his way through the ink. today we walked for 15 miles, my shadow and I, an inseparable pair. flies hitched rides in the sheltered side. miles and miles of comatose sand. miles and miles of faraway beaches like a dream-scape that you wish to keep following, a long thread that envelopes the island. a sixty-nine mile loop of gold.

a state of mind . . . or grace . . . or less . . .

zeus sits cold on the mountain, overlord with empty eyes, hardboiled and sightless, uncaring and non-judgmental. old beardy doesn't give a fuck any more. apollo/dionysus writhe through our bodies helix like, consuming each other over and over. the pagans understood this basic concept: there is no linear journey toward *utopia* or *heaven*, there is only the battle of *chaos* and *order*, each attempting to subsume the other but only managing to mutate their own essence, a constant skirmish of malleable entities. yet we define such phenomena with our child like tongues and confine each to the brevity of a single word.

a big grey cat has arrived now. squinting his eyes to see if i'm kind. A beautiful grey, striped, with golden eyes. craning its neck, staring down. maybe the cats here are friendlier than the people. there's a standoff. it leaps off the wall, soundlessly, and now it's bathing in the scent of food (sardines, big greek tomatoes, onion. a humble fare that will soak up all my beer nicely. but I must drink one more) slinks off, a new promise, he can't have any of mine anyway. *go on leave me with the lonely porch to listen to the Germans in their huge round tent.* the Greeks arguing at the bar. a background of crickets. I'd rather just have crickets. I'd rather just lie next to a true form in true love with paradise but the pipe dream is reality crushed — snuffed out by biting flies, things that sting, breathing difficulties, idiosyncrasies, my mind, your mind the fact the moment arrives and then is gone, irre-

trievable. that's why it's a mistake to go back. everything is always different — even what appears refreshingly the same.
I'm training myself to write thru the noise.

Talking of noise

all across the city they lay down a desperate tune. the inane beat of the forced art. the song you must enjoy! it trickles down the drains. on the tube they smile but in reality every note is contained within the melancholy of a raindrop. *dance* they say, gyrating crazily before you. *engage* they say, the words are simple, any idiot can join in. hold hands, expose those fleshy whites. there are pulses of enthusiasm trembling your frame . . . but didn't some woman jump up the same as the last one? the skinny one with the long straight hair. she is getting spiritual. her aura extends as far as her bank account and the material wealth she accumulates through the PR and hype.

but I tell you it is a tune born of fear, insecurity, the urge to be accepted by the throng — whose very existence is derived through FEAR. *fear* of having a voice, *fear* of stepping beyond acceptance. plumb for the safe tune. better to play it safe, the heads nod in the bar, *play something we know. something any idiot can sing along to as we drool into our pints. anyway those other songs make me feel something and I don't like it. want to be happy and dumb. stare at the girls on the dance floor. stare at the girls on the screen. entertain the fantasy. god the little bitch is hot for it.* you nod at your mates *I'd fucking shag the shit out of that* you say and they stare up nodding. doreen lost it long ago, she's putting on the pounds, fat cow rarely has a good word for anyone, and candy, well she's thin and young and wants to be a pop star but will wind up in a circle of cocks face dripping with jism. you've all got it out. you all put it in. our fat mouths. our lusting hearts, our craven minds.

down there in the holiday village, where the brits sit in their cheap-brit-culture-clubs, the swill gushes out the drainpipes. tarts hoist their skirts and watch the talent go by hoping for a holiday fuck. the reps are up and goading the sad ambience. the same tune. desperation. they sell it in bottles. desperate, like the chubby girl trying to look like a model, vacuum-packed in a stocking of silk . . . to mimic the gracelessness of some skinny singer miming words she can barely remember.

blue star naxos fading into the haze

they have given me a tiny room with a view through an alley to the ocean. a narrow strip of azure, trapped between grubby pale veils. the chinese maid is watering plants. on rooftops aerials are strapped to upturned tables and rusting artificial limbs. it's the chaos of this place that attracts me here time after time, the tumbled nature of its barnacle architecture. the way nature scours all into art with the invisible brillo pad of the wind. the old town, still part venetian, part modern, part ancient. the smell wafts up from the waterfront — souvlaki and oils, rich red sauces. thyme and sage. the evening sun delineates every facet of detail from plant and building, balcony, aerial, wire, skipping birds across rooftops, waves, coils on coils of the big ropes that hold the ferries firm against the quay. this is a kind of paradise. right now, here, at this moment, palm fingers bowing. by night they gather by the temple awaiting a pagan dusk.

all that remains of the temple of apollo is a huge stone portal. it appears to balance precariously on the remains of marble walls surely too narrow to support such an edifice. it should topple, why doesn't the dionysian wind shake it down?

Day Four

a fist fulla thieves, a filth of thieves, a mound of flies, a cavity. who knows. the old couple whose rooms these are stare at me from their living room table. old and infirm, she occasionally makes it out back with the zimmer frame. they are hushed, embarrassed. the TV is always on loud till 11 then they slumber. i am the only guest.
have you ever *never* felt part?
can't meet their eyes in the streets
everyone is smiling, dancing, they
are paired or in groups
and your loneliness is like a star
collapsing.
you long to grab someone by the arm
and in an offhand but friendly manner
explain your blues.
the terrible longing for company. but everyone *is*
in company *shining* outside their holiday bars
munching octopus, glasses clinking.
even the beach makes you sad
you watch them pass down there on the street
up here, from a hidden vault plus wine
jealous of smiles, gorgeous girlfriends
singing chefs, traditional atmospheric romantics

sitting at the temple's frame watching them
take snap shots of the dying sun
cursing them *but I clench my jaw*
and bite it,
crush it
a little ball of spittle
spat back into the void.

consumerism made the world HOLLOW

a proclaimation of the sightless eyeless legless tongueless earless care-less couldn't-care-less out there amongst the octopus char and the glittering baubles (available in every town). parading wares and snares bleached to Euro/US standards with a funky rhythm slightly ambient chorus and lyrics to reflect the freedom the liberty the self and moonlit dollars beneath the big cash tree

'come try, come buy you can't be in until you're IN!" Every facet is for sale, give them a scent and they'll slap down a price. give them a cent and they'll hike up the price! top dollar for a curious blonde, top dollar for the hint of her whim, top dollar for a smile without hooks, top dollar for an Every Ready Fuck.

Day Five

they will crawl on their hands and knees up to the church of Panagia Evangelista. past the gimmick shops with their 10' red candles, spores of crucifixes, idols and icons, tin and blue paint, garbage dressed as the real thing. these believers. those whom walk the rags laid down for the madmen (like it were a hollywood carpet) in their finest rags. dressed up for god.

you better be well dressed for the lord, you better buy a trinket or a bottle of holy water pray/ hope your moral base can save you from your children.
i could *'not care'* but as I walk the avenues, past orthodox souvenirs, the cheap tourist crap, past hordes of sea shells turned into wall hangings for dust bowl homes (it's coming believe me) well, i feel the voice begin to bite, i've a bad taste in my mouth. i crunch down the urge to yell

"I AM SATAN — I HAVE BUSINESS IN TOWN!"

spit on the virgin, de-flower her, strip away the christian shroud, reveal her as she was before. momma all mad, earth goddess mentalist, writhing on the ground with a serpent stuck up her thatch.

it's the blind belief ingrained in every plastic 'fix.
it's the bray of the herd and the scent they leave behind smells of shite. what a mess they make.

look at him they say. Look at
that
lunatic saint — Saint Migman
patron of freaks and imbeciles
they come to my cave door, offering
talismans made of chocolate and glue
sparks of genius and idiocy

some other day

ANDROS TOWN

the plastic age remnants will be dug up by inhabitants of the psionic-dream-age, and whereas they might profess poetry over a broken piece of mycenaean pottery 10 layers down, they will unearth, with a tut, another piece of the plastic age! they will sigh sadly and place it to be recycled into its original crude form.

there again the sun could melt us all tomorrow. the moon might decide never to reflect the glow again and in rejection super nova. we all have our own end, our fate etched into the weft. perhaps it is already written. perhaps the Norns know it already. that the dream repeats itself, that several lives co-exist and are merged in the subconscious pit

we face the beast and view the world through its mask. a life wish or a death wish. how do we reconcile our lives with the finality of our doom?

i shiver, a shadow at my shoulder. the mirror is there, a darker reflection looks back. a certain knowledge in the shadows. i look to the light but it burns my eyes . . . i look away.

Day 0/20

the sounds from the jukebox house are better tonight — kind of jazzy upbeat woman singing. better than last night's dirges of plop. cat fight along the street, this time it's not the children. there are lots of teenagers here, always in the throes of adolescent drama, overdosed on ham acted greek soaps.

the moon rises above a ragged pennant of cloud, silhouetting the mountain i could not climb because my back has gone. the kids below are winding up the old woman, whispering innocence. i mean there seem to be a lot of gangly male youths about, car boy types for the main, little to do in the winter save pop wheelies down the beach front. i'm the only tourist in this place and half then shops and cafes are bolted shut. so i'm cooking another tomato sauce with veg, this time some sausages too. a bottle of cheap plonk, "greek letter insert here" it says. it is in a carton and was 1.60 E. cheap bastard that i am. those galleries of light keep slipping out, seems to liven up at this hour, then come 11 everything stops. different from spain where at 11 everything is just getting going in that loud brash love of *'la vida'* spanish style.

i can't wait to find a place to write awhile, to extricate this fucking noise, the white noise of my soul. even before i hit santorini (seems far off — like a dream to come). just can't wait to get fired into it, feel juicy, ideas, promises — but here no. too much many old women shouting at nuisance kids and that old sad eyed dog moping on. the canines here are all desperate for attention. came across one hitched to a rusty old barrel by a thick length of rope up the mountain trail. poor bastard nearly choked to death when i made to leave. something about a whining dog, like sandpaper rubbed beneath the skin. somewhere. reminds me of mexico, those mangy wrecks little more than scabs on legs, fly paper skin, crusted around sores and in amongst the pustuled-hairless-redness a pair of eyes, those sad, longing *i-want-you to-stroke-me-human* eyes, but you have to look away, avoid the hook or you'll have to kick the little bastard up the arse! horrible, horrible for the poor creature, but mainly for how it (the sight, the rejecting) makes us feel. unless you're a callous type who hates animals. suddenly I hear the greyman, one time as we sat with a bottle of buckfast, at the back of a bus to glasgow, just before the bus driver warned us, after the bottle of buckfast gathered momentum down the aisle. He shouted "*make the world vegetarian -kill all the animals!*"

another soap opera scene. voices raised, doors slam man walks over to car, red lights glow, he's off — to the taverna to get blitzed on raki. Well someone's still pissed down there, woman sounding off shit, we're back to dance beats.

if i could choose anywhere to be right now, i'd be on top of that ragged crown up there. piss drunk on the skull of old blind zeus. if it were still and mild, i can imagine seeing the whole island (you can from up there they tell me) by moonlight, shimmering on the ocean all around! can we take these moments with us when we go? do they come round again, as our physical bodies break down, do the dispersing chemicals release these fragments of captured moments, only real to us, only poignant to us? And perhaps in that instant eternal moments are ultimately experienced.

today as i sat here in the evening i watched a flying insect, an overgrown mosquito of some kind, flying crazily, neurotically we might say, side to side, jerking wildly as though when released from larval form it had found its wings and the sudden burst of energy sent it wild on a lunatic flight into the great blue — or a swallows beak. and i thought *what is the point?* Even if the bird doesn't its life span is so short, it spends most of its time as a blind grub in the stomach of a dead cat. as far as i see it's a brief luxury for such important waste disposal work.

there will come a day when one of those insects will hop out of some recently devoured carcass into the mouth of a passing jogger and an infectious disease will wipe 75% of us out. i can hear my father wringing his hands in expectation, jumping up and down around his one friend and enemy — TV. i can almost see the hunch of bile on his back, that hump has weighted him down all these years, but i can imagine it deflating, like a silage spreader as he twirls in ecstasies of doom. maybe he is right to feel like that. i mean not only are we littering the land with debris of our everyday lives we are littering with our houses. everywhere i go it's the same! spain, greece, beattock! you hear the government lackeys preach "*more housing, need more housing!*" but i thought the sperm count was falling! or is that no one wants to live on-top-of-each-other anymore? well the poor will have to (affordable housing) but the rich, well the countryside is now their playground, as it is their Med. look at these islands, the development is fairly low key but untidy. the majority of the dwellings are empty most of the year, second homes for foreigners and athenians. it must be strange for a local, to wind up living in a town that is dead and devoid of life for 8 or 9 months. wouldn't it be better for the property and local economies if the place was leased out to others for part of the year? agencies could handle it. artist retreats, seasonal workers, I mean winter in greece is preferable to winter in Edinburgh — am I right? oh, i know I am.

okay, here's a paranoid thought tossed randomly (started with a thought of the moon) — why do flies always seem to like me? i've always known i've the blood type that attracts biters, but flies, they're always hanging around and yesterday on the bus one flitted around my legs and tickled my ears and I thought *is there a smell of death around me? am I rotting already? are they hatching out of me? my bloated gut is filled with writhing balls of white maggots!* isn't it only a matter of time till a grey doctor passively informs me that i'm already dead and I explode into a roaring terminus of bluebottles?

mid morning thoughts, the kind of thing that plagues my mind at 3 am. well, at least this rooftop abode comes equipped with TV and there is a stripper call girl channel where beautiful athenian tarts strip. yes, at least there is this. beauty plus lust equals a series of spasmodic jerks, maybe some drool and a brief, though satisfying, ejaculation into some toilet roll.
they are playing that cranberries song. i wonder who is playing it. another one hit wonder. whatever happened to queen dolores? destroyed by the media mincer i guess. however there was something quintessentially irish about them, as oppose U2 whom i abhor with a pure, instinctive reaction since i was a kid. Never mind, just fancies, follies, rooftop meanderings as the surf scuds in and the cold breeze flurries down the mountain. the moon is nearly in sight. one day that same disc might rise over the exact same mountain only there will be no lights, no music, no children hissing like cats, no smells of cooking, no angst ridden teens . . . only a silence that no one will hear.

Day 24

wandering the old town her ghost got me. walked and found bays, soft sand to sink in, water is still fine. brisk strokes. fishermen out in the bay loading up their nets. these past times, the ocean of memories, surface like dolphins through pools of oil, like blue plastic bags. in each of us the line goes deep. moments, times, events, all relative, all linked by the track lines we have taken, choices decisions, accident, fate — the vikings had the Norns frantically weaving the tapestry of destiny, what would they use now? something synthetic, maybe computer software, something funky and chic looking. my choice tonight is an important one. history will alter because of it — where should i eat? what to eat and what to drink while eating this eat. yes friends, it has come to this.

the shrill of a cricket, close, down by the swimming pool, a cautionary note. they say that the noise is the sound of their legs. a stupid and unsubstantiated nonsense. that chirpy sound is the male cricket hammering away on his tiny manhood, having a right good speedy wank — fast, count the oscillations! the female, with bated breath, waits and watches, fascinated, finally shivering off her shyness they will copulate for hours down by the pool

did we ever copulate for hours by the pool? no, i don't think so — god i wish I were a cricket!

the air is char grilled

sometimes i bask in the glow of not being in scotland. not being in the UK is what i should say. scotland is ruined by being part of that hideous nanny state monster. no, despite my gripes about litter and religion, which, let's face could be any cuntry really. no, time i sit and listen to the happy voices of the greeks in the ouzeria, savouring the char grilled air. the waves, the crickets, the chaotic paintwork on the building opposite, the gentle air of neglect. for despite the tourism these guys know, deep inside they are only building ruins. that they already build on ruins! if only they cleared away the debris (every country should do this) then what a place! *que bueno!*

all these connections, all just waiting to hang ourselves on each other. do you know what i mean mr. super nova man? you met a girl on a random train and chained your heart or your lust to her. as i move (slowly, ever slowly) through grease, sorry greece, i meet randomly these beautiful women, make contacts, get addresses and i wonder, if i wanted surely i could stick my neck into one of these silken nooses. let them draw me tight, legs kicking as they suck the passion from my mouth.

is this what it's about? stick it in and pull it out, do the hokey pokey and turn around, is that what it's all about?

i have friends who maintain BREED! sure, propagation of the species, to what end? to overrun like rabbits in australia — ah but man you can't compare us to animals — no? then how about a virus, an infectious spread that curses the world, a rapacious greedy animal-virus that wipes out anything else for fun? how long before we exterminate sea gulls because they gobble up what's left of marine reserves? yet we are solely to blame for depleting them — with our huge brains and self control! *don't make me fucking laugh.*

ghost

you stole upon me. lost in the old town i saw you sitting by the chapel still working on that beautiful sketch. you were there. i felt the well of loneliness open up and i stamped my foot. clenched my jaw. in the tiny museum next to the orthodox cathedral (1.50E) where icons of half ripped faces clotted the old beams, black worm eaten wood.

beautiful yet it reflected the hierarchal nature of religion — christ the high priest beast in gowns and robes and all the images of fear pyramids with eyes and mystification of alpha to omega etc. the toad at the reception croaked occasionally, regarded at me seedily, licking his frog lips. who picked him I think, who picked him?

the fly is trapped upon the thin skin of the surface, held there by the tension . . . and it is doomed. it tries to escape, legs kicking helplessly but it only succeeds only in propelling itself in clockwise circles, creating a lovely triskele of rippled motion, terminating each flurry in an explosion of minute ripples. it rests then moves in clockwise motion. as its strength weakens the dances become shorter. until it is drowned.

nothing stirs. there are no shadows. boats trail the fluid soundless. the cloud hangs, suspended shoals above. the masts remain rigid. evening brings the deep water fishes hungry for bait. hungry for the plate. this is winter's breath. these shrinking daylight hours. the darkness seeps in with the silhouettes of cats.

Day 30

Samos

ah — there's nothing like the smell of tetramethrin piperonyl butoxide in the evening. *Die fucker die!*

hotel pythagoras has seen better days. a block that can't be more than 30 or 40 years old. typical of the concrete substructure dwellings that still proliferate the greek islands. a characterless building. cold terrazzo floors, crumbling balconies, flaky paint, damp. on one wall we have stippled picture of marilyn monroe — the type that foundation art students conjure for mediocre assignments in drawing styles. of course, it's a mirror too, adding to the tackiness. other wall typical painting for tourists of greek landscape. rendering in a style you can find throughout the med. the scene depicts the ocean, a wave coming in, a rowing boat on the sand (looks like it's floating) reflecting some peachy glow in the fading/hazy sun. there are patches of little clouds, seagulls reeling about, although they could also be kite surfers, glimpsed through bamboo cane and dunes. all condensed within fake rustic white washed frame. that's the decor. downstairs the bespectacled owner always smiles when you ask him something, but I suspect he hates the place and all the people in it. i guess there are semi-permanent relics living here, including old women glued to TV downstairs watching subtitled american soaps and two Indians who sell leather belts — add to this to scores of lingering mosquitoes and a pair of grey waist coated crows who crawk in the tree that obscures my balcony view, well there you go.

so then what next?

i'd just vandalised the hotel chairs
white juice singing in my veins
hunger bade me "out"
but i couldn't move

"insanity in a temporary room can only
be temporary" says the 6 foot crow
with the face of marilyn monroe

"insanity is a parched beach waiting tides
to return"
"very pro-found" i snarled
to the reflection trapped in lemon
circles.

it turned, looked me square in the eye
its beak parted. "crakka Caw
cka cka!" It recited.
"okay" i reasoned, "that being said
you don't know and no one does
and you being a projection of some
inner psychological reasoning well . . . "
"no, i'm real. As real as."
and that's when we danced
slow trope round the room
his marilyn eyes stripping me up and down
though fixed to the platter
the feast to come.

Day 31.75

Hotel Pythagoras with lust in the groin and playboy at hand

what girls? where are the fucking girls? it's all adverts, adverts, articles (in greek) of history, personalities, football teams, chic lifestyle wannabes, playboys . . . *where are the tarts?* i mean 'models', yeah, whatever, there i am, throbbing member in hand turning the page after page of rolex, peugeot, christ! *I'm going soft!* what a waste of 8 euros, I'd be better off making shadow puppets with my free hand. all this for a simple momentary ejaculation. this one thing we hanker for. with woman, or partner, or without. the phallic temples of old are there to remind us it has always been this way. the phallic missiles of ultimate extinction are there to remind us it's here to finality. it is after all a man's world and the best women can do is pull on pants and don a suit or lay back and act like you 'like it'.

the storm hangs banners of obsequious black cloud over the town, the bay, the mountains. the rain echoes the emptiness. a coolness that settles in the soul, cold on the ocean roaring in the darkness. reading failed states by chomsky, seems the mood is set. makes my blood ice. these pious two-faced leaders, the NWO, self appointed trustees of the world — how do they sleep? as self professed christians how do they manage to lift their eyes to the camera and tell these hideous lies without convulsing in shame and begging forgiveness of their mild and gentle shepherd? the world is in peril. what chance have we in the face of such adversity? the face of such evil, dressed in monkey suits reciting their doctored rhetoric of deceit. these good guys slinging their cowboy shots with a gunslinger stance. like that scene in dr. strange love, the cowboy riding the nuke like a bucking bronco down into oblivion. it's enough to make you think *'what's the point?'*. no wonder the kids swarm towards nihilism. i felt the same at their age after our daily dose of the 6pm news over dinner. weeks go by and i don't even glance at a headline. i adopt the stance of it's better not to know, the same as the vast swathes of the population all over the world do. even those who once tried to change things have seen that their attempts amount to little. we lose ourselves in fantasy, video games, digital head trips longing to avoid that which is glaring us all in the face — the total inevitability of nuclear conflict, the annihilation of human, animal, plant, insect life forms and the end of history, the close of time, the death of fragile earth by our own hand. by our own magnanimous power crazed hand.

so what for a society that demands we settle, get kids, get the house, get a fixture, contribute? and those who've put themselves in that position but deep down aren't happy are madly jealous of the way people like me live. their silence speaks like thunder on a sunny day. it manifests itself in cryptic little comments like "oh, oh you're getting on . . . how old are you now?" we must all fight these conventions, all of us. it is such blind acceptance of enforced and so-called 'natural' paradigms that have gotten us into the abyss we are in. there is still time to struggle free. we needn't plunge into the void. it is we, the people who can and must make a difference. we just have to go about numerous and different ways of achieving this. we are up against a faceless wall of concrete, but in each crack, each crevice, roots take hold, weeds grow, flowers bloom, trees take hold, the roots weaken the walls
we must weaken this wall.

it comes . . . I can feel the wall shiver. Expectation. Here things change . . . seeds take hold.

Day 33

6 or 7 hours to wait. listening to the screech of the crane as the cables resist and crunch their pulleys and moorings. big lorries sweep along the coast road behind me. they sound like jets coming in. and always the endless slap of waves against a shingle beach. washing up blue plastic bottle tops. the sky is grey, threatening to rain. another long day. last night I bailed on instinct, it didn't feel right, with that tin-can shaking all about and all those saturated faces pretending it's all okay, with illness, with profound sickness. the worried eyed son and his mother on deck, counting out the minutes, cold, hungry, sick like hell, an eternity of lobbing about, lurching side to side listening to things clank and clump below. the lights of the mountain town that were like glowing pellets sprinkled on the slopes lurched crazily through the window adding to the general disorientation.

i'm crazy, all this talk of fate and destiny and that stone I carved to try out, sun and the moon — it just is. like the little fishing boat pulling out into the grey sea, it just is. fated or not. just is. what can it change? and yet i want to affect change. i want to save the world! but how does one deal with the impotency you feel when there seems to be no way to implement what you consider 'reasonable' change? is the populace so stunned? is it the path they have chosen or the elite (destruction, annihilation) so irreversible? when does the background buzz become a roar?

it will take 5-6 hours to reach naxos (a rough estimation). it's raining, a constant pour, occasionally getting excited enough to downpour for a few minutes. even made a phone call somewhere, everywhere else the same as it always seems to be — in stasis! i can imagine skies as grey as these but for weeks, a cold wind, a wind that drives the moisture into your bones. the hopeless greens and the grey. don't worry, i will return, i have to. an old man passes on a bike "too much raining too much raining today." he says as he trundles by. flies crawling around table edge on my legs, rain dripping through the bamboo veranda shade out there, like a leaking faucet. loud fishermen explaining things to each other with exaggerated movements, like charades. stays like this i'll have to buy a coat. feel damp, clammy on the shoulders. On the deck last night i became invisible in my hoody and the wind blew straight through.

SUCK EGGS CUNT

all the gardens were particular and the owners' pussies perpendicular and "*oh what splendour how culturific*" adaptability — i suppose some beast of diction pissed over sentiment and channeled into pop tune vernacular, ah so spectacular to witness proto culture as modern as a whore a groaning cube of cunts and cocks all with faces in the too right places, anon dread for newly wed celebs with tone deaf hearts and gucci shirts never any holes and too much soul proclaiming *individuality* — by proxy sure, a nice big car, a fenced in nest, i'm alright and fuck the rest. Billboard pimps source billboard whores "*all the others do you'd be sorry not to.*" a spanking conservatory, a shiny new box to speed through the lane now that you are free.

Day again

Naxos again

last night i stuffed myself rotten.

a) 5 — 8pm 1 and half litre white wine

b) 8;30 restaurant: bacon stuffed with aubergine with a tomato and mint sauce on a bed of chips. this would have been enough as it is. i also gulped down a 1 litre bottle of cold mineral water during meal.

c) 9.20ish main course — big plate of spaghetti with mussels, prawns and chopped seafood sticks, picking at it coz suddenly i'm bloated but i want to eat because it looks good — bit salty, mussels must be frozen, chewy, then i can't finish it. i ask for the bill, waitress brings me courtesy dessert of sponge cake — i feel bad but i have to refuse — i need to get the fuck out of there fast — I'm going to explode — my chest is expanding, my guts swollen and painful. i feel like someone put a chunk of ice inside me. So i pay, don't wait for change and get the fuck out man, hit the room, lie on the bed just groaning. oh fuck, fuck, then toilet projectile vomit — torrents of tomatoes and chewed potatoes, still warm, direct into the bowl. i get back into the bed, man, it doesn't taste bad! tastes okay second time round. So i switch on TV some old flick with marlon as a colonel in US army, hilarious end flashing between man he just shot, screaming women on bed and marlon stroking his jaw looking slightly perplexed. coughed up a chunk of spaghetti, went to sleep.

Ack ack ack

Ioninnia, or something like that.

a parade of lights. a parade of 'cool' troops of army boys and jets flying over. Suddenly hit, overwhelmed by the madness of the world. all this motion. 3 wheeled carts a donkey passing a billboard 10' Greek letters "BUY
ME, SUCK ME DRY" shops full of fake icons, tik tak beads and evil eyes. One throws down his zimmerframe and dives
across the street. Myceanean coin from fortress banks' depository
of instant cash. who's who who's in the know? a mobile phone better have a decent ringtone. you better have the names and a face to match look wrong, we'll stare, smirk at you from behind our manicured claws.

dark face drunk bitter in the crowd beneath parasol lights his plastic bags clink doom laden, sure, a sideway lurching line into the blackest lonliest maw of night. pick-ups with smoky windows loitering with warming engines revving as the tight legs pass, throbbing as the bell skirts pass. Voices all around, a man drunken laughing like a child sobbing brought to tears by flickering text over
raki. laughter that ripples out the open bar door like a madman stroking the finer keys. Scarves and big bags nearly Xmas, first sight of Santa; santa cola, viva los cabrones advertising in 10' english reads "LIVING GOOD THE GOOD WAY" with picture of a thin girl like all these
thin girls with scissor legs and perfect dress sense but naught but crosses in their eyes, Xs, 'fixes, all the bullshit, all the drama, all the lies swallowed in tabular form daily. Where are the young punks? Is there any dissent in the provinces? have they truly won? so that by the shoreline you gaze loftily at mountain peaks feeling justified and so alive ignoring the plastic sludge squishing beneath your manicured toes? there is no singular truth, so lets just deal in facts (the
multi-eyed creator form is a great un-shape of truths, each eye blazing

forth its own flavour) . all these fucking motors, all these big fat shiny's, cocks plugged into feel the piston, we're addicted and mouthing "freedom" oily
and "individuality" know thyself — behind the wheel of your unchoice. make me laugh why don't you.

A mash of Hours

there it is. the sum of my intelligence. all this wandering, hornets caged in the span of my middle brain. there it is, the summation — a fat puke into a porcelain gourd. a big fat ZERO . . . but then that's at least still something . . . perhaps it's the main thing. and you, drifting in and out of some hazed stupor, did you glean anything from this? a tiny light, a little death, a stifled yawn? the road stretches on. it looks endless. but i'm sure that it will terminate (in a blaze of screams) one day, at some point. we are all in that one same boat, our paths are best kept in solitude and the occasional, hearty geyser of vomit.

ST. migman, somewhere else

Dave Migman recently fled Greece and currently lives in Edinburgh, Scotland. His first book, *The Wolf Stepped Out* (a grim exposé of foetal Ballet rackets), is also published by Dog Horn Publishing.

Quimby Melton

Ghidorah Attacks!

Modern narrative's three-headed monster

The concept of pure art — pure poetry, pure painting, and so on — is not entirely without meaning; but it refers to an aesthetic reality as difficult to define as it is to combat. In any case, even if a certain mixing of the arts remains possible, like the mixing of genres, it does not necessarily follow that they are all fortunate mixtures. There are fruitful cross-breedings which add to the qualities derived from the parents; there are attractive but barren hybrids and there are likewise hideous combinations that bring forth nothing but chimeras.

— Andre Bazin, "In Defense of Mixed Cinema" (1952)

"Reports of my death have been greatly exaggerated."

As a graduate student who studied the novel, I took great pleasure in proclaiming the genre's death. Of course, academics generally prefer studying sedate archaeological relics. But like all human beings, I'm also bound to torture, and even kill, the things I love because doing so has the potential to make me master of that which has mastery over me. Violent resistance to tyranny, even in its softer forms, is fundamental to the human experience, it seems. And so it was for me, with the novel, back then.

Lacking any cultural capital whatsoever, I naively fantasized about writing an essay I'd publish simultaneously in the *NYRB*, *LRB*, and the *L.A. Times*. Channeling some sort of opium-crazed Symbolist poet, I imagined it beginning:

When I walk into Barnes & Noble, I feel as if I've stepped into a giant necropolis — a reeking mausoleum dedicated to the great art form of the 19th century — that wouldn't be worth the trip if it didn't sell CDs, coffee, and especially movies.

A pretentious argument, too clever by half, would follow, encouraging people, like a blood-crazed Italian Futurist, to let the old novel rot and endorsing the mechanical flicker as the narrative genre of the future. But just as the mechanized killing of WWI revealed the jejune flaws of Futurism, and thereby shut it up for good, I too found myself illuminated and my opinions altered by a certain event.

I think my silly idea that film had somehow displaced the novel had its origins in a misreading of the "Photography, Film, and the Novel" section of Michael McKeon's *Theory of the Novel* and an over-eager, simultaneous inhalation of Walter Benjamin's famous essays "The Storyteller" and "The Work of Art in the Age of Mechanical Reproduction." After my initial exposure to these, I became convinced that the title "Great Narrative Genre" had passed from novel to film, just as the novel had once received it from the epic poem, and that film would preside over the death of the novel, just as the novel had watched the epic poem more or less fade into history. While Benjamin's Marxism all but ensures he'd advocate this type of transposition, rereading McKeon one day I realized I'd substantially misunderstood his take on the subject. With a cartoonish slap to my forehead, it dawned on me that Benjamin's seductive ruminations, my own leftist tendencies, and my id's excitement at the prospect of raining merciless salvos on my great love had all caused me to project overtones of displacement onto the history of narrative generally and, more specifically, McKenon's suggestion that we can conceive of "film as a radical extension of the novel." But really, this isn't what McKeon or any number of other film, novel, and narrative theorists mean at all. Instead, they most likely use *extension* in a more strictly denotative way, that is, to suggest film adds to and expands the genre boundaries of the novel.

Mercifully enlightened by this point of view, I'm immensely grateful that my little essay combusted in the planning stages and that, like the terrible Ghidorah looming over Japan, this essay emerged from its piss-fuming ashes.

It seems natural, however lamentable, that my mind would give Benjamin's legion of words dominion over McKeon's elegantly effective handful. I can forgive myself for this. Coming to such a wrongheaded conclusion, though, also means I temporarily took leave of my Bakhtin: something I'm rather ashamed of having done. An intellectual superhero, the old Russian reminds us in "Epic and the Novel" that mapping the novel's perimeter is more or less a fool's errand and that while the genre may change forms and gobble up other genres, **THE NOVEL**, true to its adjectival origins, remains just that. (And as someone who famously used the only remaining pages from a lost manuscript to roll cigarettes, one can say with some certainty that comrade Bakhtin practiced a form of the textual versatility he preached!) Therefore, like a royal courtier bowing before a new monarch, even if we are of the opinion that the novel has somehow died or been dislodged, we can't really bid it adieu with any more finality than, "The novel is dead. Long live the novel." What the genre is and what the genre isn't, what defines it and what we exclude from such definitions, when it began and when it will merge with the infinite — these are all questions contemporary genre studies wrestle with and questions individuals and interpretive communities must ultimately answer for themselves.

As interested parties since Aristotle have known, such questions also complicate our ability to taxonomize any genre, let alone the wildly interactive, 21st-century phyla of kingdom narrative. But we dedicated literary and celluloid Linnaeans continue delusively separating the specimens of our analysis, and the products of our labor, into exclusive categories nevertheless, even as the lines separating the genre identities of novels and films have broken down in remarkable and daresay unprecedented ways. Of course, novels and films are both narrative forms and have, as a result, an essential consanguinity regardless of their distinctive structural elements and unique codes of inherent information. But I would suggest an even more intimate connection has developed between the two, a bond that makes these structures and codes functionally irrelevant in the 21st century. So like a sebaceous carnival caller drawing back a curtain and inviting his audience to gasp at the circus' prize freak, I suggest we have a three-headed narrative monster in our midst: one that's part novel, part film, and part intermediary screenplay; one that has become, and will likely continue to serve as, the dominant narrative genre of our time. And I invite one and all to step right up and marvel at this strange and unusual anomaly, this mutant oddity, this aberration.

I assure you, ladies and gentlemen, you won't believe your eyes!

It's alive!

While most people wouldn't have any trouble distinguishing a performance art "happening" from a Verdi opera, it would nevertheless be decidedly Platonic to suggest genre taxonomy is airtight. As such, doing so has been decidedly out of fashion since at least the Enlightenment. Thinkers from that time on have outlined different theories of genre interactivity, subjectivity, and mutability, including the late Jacques Derrida, who argues in "The Law of Genre" that texts participate in rather than belong to certain genres, and UVa's Ralph Cohen, who argues in "History and Genre" that genres are open categories that change and decline for historical reasons. Moreover, poets like Baudelaire and novelists like Hermann Broch gave us "prose poems" and "lyrical novels," respectively: compounds that obfuscate what it means to be a member of either constituent class. My cretinous idea that film would, and likely already had, displaced the novel operated around the earlier, Platonic concept of genre integrity: a fallacy that also drives carpal-tunnel book-types like myself and mole-eyed film-folk to segregate their novels and films into functionally exclusive genre classes. This line of thinking not only assumes (a) the credible existence of genre exclusivity and (b) the more or less absolute integrity of each genre's individual province. Like a Texas Baptist, it also discounts the possibility of evolution. Who's to say, after all, that *Paradise Lost* isn't just a versified proto-novel or that *Forrest Gump* isn't just a jazzed-up oral narrative? Moreover, readers consistently interpret novels like Joyce's *Ulysses* and Woolf's *Mrs. Dalloway* as modern lyrical epics rendered in a poetic, subjective style of prose called "free indirect discourse." Therefore, even though it's hardly uncommon for narrative genres to overlap and evolve, I would argue the contemporary relationship that has evolved between film and the novel is rather unique. Partnered and antagonistic, fused and disjoined — the monstrous, three-headed narrative genre formed by the novel, screenplay, and film operates and exists despite the constituent genres' chronological and temporal differences and the dissimilarity of the mechanical processes by which they operate in the world.

Acutely sensitive to this illogical partnership between novel and film, the extremist constituency of the textual interest group often discusses the modern connections between textual novels and motion picture films with dramatic lamentations. Tapping into the old text-smart, graphic-stupid opposition all too common in the Occident, they lament both the dumbing down of culture generally and, more specifically, the brutalization of "their" novels by "uncaring" filmmakers guilty only of the abridgment necessitated by "their" genre. Such arguments amount to little more than hot air, though, as even the most marmish librarians, Romance-novel-obsessed mothers, Hollywood-wary preachers, and dedicated English majors like to turn Ludovico patient and "viddy the old films now and again." And when filmmakers like Merchant Ivory Productions turn one of their beloved novels, "classic" or otherwise, into a film, woe be unto the plebes who dare cut in line at the box office. Perhaps nothing illustrates this ironic hypocrisy better than the *Harry Potter* phenomenon of the past decade. In grand Hebraic tradition, notorious critics of visual culture routinely praise J. K. Rowling's books, widely crediting them with "getting kids to read again." But as anyone could have anticipated, the currency-ejaculating popularity of this novel series proved irresistible to Hellenic film producers. And, in due course, the books were turned into an ongoing sequence of wildly successful films that has been rabidly consumed by readers of the books.

The bookish set need not worry too much, though. While the monstrous partnership between contemporary novels and films isn't likely to cease any time soon, it doesn't represent an outright fusion of the genres, nor does it threaten to extinguish or displace the novel as I once believed. As I suggest, other genres do rather effortlessly melt into one another, forming delicious melanges. Writing a prose poem, for example, can be as simple as dropping rhyme, adding narrative, and increasing the objectivity of the voice. Likewise, lyricizing a novel mostly involves dolling up the narration, adding a few extra metaphors, and spiking the subjective flavor of the characters. Films and novels, though, do not compliment as effortlessly or as logically. In fact, rather immovable realities separate textual novels and motion picture films and make them as ultimately incongruous as a zoophilic rustic and the ovine object of his desire. But like that rustic, narrative creators, businesspeople, and consumers seem to desperately want the two to come together. And like mad scientists, our desire to create this hodgepodge narrative mass has forced a grotesque and distorted match and succeeded only in creating a mutually affective relationship between constituents that hasn't, and likely cannot and will not, lead to full fusion or displacement. Fleshy bits of each genre's individual identity remain on the semi-coagulated whole. And unlike prose poems and lyrical novels, the novel-film genre compound doesn't represent a congruous, harmonious synthesization at all. Instead, it defies taxonomy, refuses to fully amalgamate the traits of its constituent narrative forms, and even necessitated the birth of the mutant screenplay to bridge the divide between novel and film. Our wild desire, therefore, has given birth to a three-headed genre monster that looms unchallenged over contemporary narrative production and consumption.

Unlike previous centuries when one genre more or less dominated kingdom narrative — e.g., the novel in the nineteenth century and the mystery play in Medieval Europe — I would argue that the preeminent genre of modern narrative is neither film nor the novel operating independently of one another. Instead, I would argue it's this three-headed genre compound. Like Ghidorah and Cerberus, fused into one body but with three distinctively snapping heads, no matter what fundamental differences exist between text and graphic, novel and film, it seems more and more inappropriate to discuss novels and films outside the context of one another. Indeed, whatever membrane(s) might have plausibly segregated these two particular narrative genres began to erode as soon as film emerged in the latter years of the 19th century. In fact, I'd put the origins of this coming-together no later than the early 1900s.

In 1915, D. W. Griffith directed an infamous movie version of Thomas Dixon's *The Clansman* he called *The Birth of a Nation*. In 1922, F. W. Murnau made a uniquely Teutonic, unauthorized film version of Bram Stoker's novel *Dracula* titled *Nosferatu: A Symphony of Horror*. And in 1924, the great proto-auteur Erich von Stroheim gave the world its ultimate director's cut: a 16+ hour long, word-for-word cinematic adaptation of Frank Norris's *McTeague* entitled *Greed*. Such early films helped established the adaptation imperative that lies at the heart of the novel-screenplay-film genre compound, and by 1968, it was so firmly entrenched in narrative culture that Alistair MacLean found himself writing the novel and screenplay versions of *Where Eagles Dare* more or less simultaneously! (Marguerite Duras, of course, did similar things with *India Song* and *Destroy, She Said*.)

Without the development and enthusiastic adoption of this imperative by filmmakers and, eventually, novelists, it's hard to see why novels and films wouldn't have pursued more parallel paths. As Henry James' cruel theatre study illustrates, novels and plays, the precursor of film, rarely intersect. Nevertheless, as I suggest, nearly all genres interact from time to time, and the same is true of even more disparate discourses. Ivan Albright painted a real-life *Picture of Dorian Gray*; Rimbaud wrote his color-based "Sonnet des voyelles"; and Debussy long planned, though never finished, more than thirty minutes of an operatic treatment of Poe's "Fall of the House of Usher." But while such instances of crossover do commonly occur, the relationships formed by the constituents don't often fundamentally undermine the core sense of what it means to be a poem, an opera, a novel, a painting, etc. Neither do these various artistic forms enter into relationships often enough that the adaptation of one by another seems natural and self-evident (however absurd this is).

It's not enough, then, to brush off the contemporary novel-film relationship with a terse, "All genres and discourses interact," because while they do, these other examples of genre interplay seem more like lender-borrower relationships than incorporating ones. Even more importantly, they lack the sort of rabid adaptation imperative that drives the assimilative intercourse characterizing the relationship between modern novels and films. Indeed, the singular belief that novels and films must interact — imperatively, consistently — frames the relationship as a sort of adaptation tango whose *colgada* and *ganchos* blur the very lines separating the genres, their profound mechanical, formal, and experiential differences be damned!

Nearly a century after the productions of Griffith, Murnau, and Stroheim initiated this awkward though indefatigable dance, novels and films have more or less totally overlapped into a developmental continuum and siamese partnership every bit as uncanny and bizarre as it is functional (and uncanny and bizarre precisely because it is so functional). *The Golden Bowl, The Great Gatsby, Gone with the Wind, The Maltese Falcon, Dune, The Da Vinci Code* — these are but a few famous examples of an astoundingly long list of novels that have been adapted into (in)famous films. (Wikipedia breaks this list into two sprawling web pages. See "List of film remakes.") Moreover, in the heyday of the studio system, Hollywood engaged famous novelists like William Faulkner and Scott Fitzgerald as literary sorcerers, charging them with turning novels into screenplays that could then be turned into films by directors. Though this practice has changed substantially — directors and professional screenwriters usually produce scripts nowadays, and novelists and playwrights infrequently adapt their own work let alone the work of others — presently, in the early twenty-first century, the practice of translating novels into films is more than commonplace. It's institutionalized, expected, and routine.

Movie rights are often negotiated simultaneously with or as part of publishing contracts for, or in anticipation of, blockbuster sequels, sophomore attempts by writers such as Charles Frazier, and late-career masterworks by writers like Cormac McCarthy and Philip Roth. And while films are frequently made without novelistic precedent, every bestseller is virtually guaranteed to be made into a movie. This has effectively repositioned the creative writing graduates pouring out of English departments as R&D laborers and market testers for their film school contemporaries. Appropriating Edward Albee, literary "Abmaphids" and "Abmafays" create the narratives that, upon being proven in the marketplace, are adapted into movies by film Abmafays lucky enough to have found professional positions in their industry (and eager to ensure theses positions continue by cashing in on the fruitful forays of said novelists). While members of the former category might resent this characterization, it would be difficult to argue against it. And even the most traditionally minded novelist would have to admit his/her position in the marketplace has radically changed when compared to that of his/her predecessors of a century and a half ago precisely because of the contemporary relationship that exists between the publishing industry and Hollywood. But lest I portray literary types as nicely paid but underappreciated laborers, there seems to be no higher compliment or validation a novel and its creator can receive than adaptation by a major motion picture studio. If lucky enough to have been thusly anointed, a writer will invariably feature the fact prominently on his/her personal website and tout it in the relevant press. And as if this weren't enough recognition, writer and publisher routinely recreate, and perhaps downgrade, adapted novels into something resembling advertising placards. They re-release texts that have been cinematized with movie poster covers and prominent badges that scream, "Now a Major Motion Picture!" Such practices can't help but make novels seem less like the comparatively self-contained, self-sufficient genre of old and more like cinematic zygotes that are sold less as literary objects and more as buzz generators for motion pictures.

In this way, modern novels essentially serve as the first treatments in a linear narrative procession that leads directly to the *telos* of the silver screen. But it works both ways. Successful movies are routinely "novelized," that is, sent backward along the more commonly trod continuum to the bookshelf. More than just an effort to cash in on a successful flickering narrative, this practice might seem decadent, extraneous, and even silly if it didn't reveal the degree to which producers, writers, and publishers have apparently begun thinking of novels and movies as fundamentally paired objects. It's one thing, after all, to parlay the paltry millions generated by a best-selling novel into tens and even hundreds of millions of dollars at the box office. This is just good American business sense. But recreating contemporary films into novels, when the receipts and audience numbers of the former dwarf those of even the most popular novel, seems grounded in some imperative other than business. To me, the phenomenon suggests that even modern movies have a sense of incompleteness without novelized versions of themselves. The (un)conscious imperative must be satisfied, it seems, and the three-headed narrative monster must be recreated, its uncontested rule in the culture and marketplace reinforced again and again whether one proceeds from page to screen or screen to page.

Finally, the contemporary relationship between novels and films isn't just "external," or business based, as it were. It can be structural and formal as well since the narratives represented by each genre often blur, interact, and conceptually overlap to the point that novel versions and film versions of a given story coalesce into a sort of cubist super-genre. Where the integral genre lines of a given narrative begin and where they end; what the audience considers legitimate and illegitimate characters, dialogue, narration and plot points; the mental record one makes of a given story with novel, film, and perhaps screenplay versions rattling around in his/her head — modern narratives that exist in novel, screenplay, and film forms can't help but become rather conceptually distorted and exponentially complicated. Of course, most people do not read screenplays — which can themselves differ profoundly from the finished films for which they serve as narrative scaffolding — and simply deal with the cognitive dissonance created by competing film and novel versions of a given narrative by opining, "The movie wasn't as good as the book." This response, though, is just a dodge for those who want to relieve their anxiety and get on with their lives. Unrepentant, die-hard narrative junkies like myself who refuse to take the easy out — and who eagerly consume screenplays to better chart the beguiling course of narrative alchemy — can't really discuss a given narrative that exists in novel, screenplay, and film versions in terms of constituent genre. Instead, the monstrous distortions of a disharmoniously unified, three-headed genre seizes our minds, each of this monster's heads contributing its own roar to the overwhelming cacophony of its existence. In this way, the novel-screenplay-film genre compound facilitates and even encourages the narratives represented by its elemental genres to outgrow their limitations and come together in a distorted whole that defies traditional genre characterization.

A Clockwork Orange gives us a concrete example of this phenomenon.

In his 1962 novel, Anthony Burgess does not give protagonist Alex a last name. However, Alex does often ascribe certain epithets to himself. For example, when seducing "two young ptitsas" into having a freaky three-way with him in a record shop, Alex refers to himself as "Alexander the Large": "I felt the old tigers leap in me and then I leapt on these two young ptitsas. This time they thought nothing fun and stopped creeching with high mirth, and had to submit to the strange and weird desires of Alexander the Large . . . "

In his masterful 1971 film version of *Clockwork*, critics think Stanley Kubrick used this line as the basis for Alex's surname "de Large" which the protagonist uses toward the end of the first act. Interestingly, Burgess didn't resist this creative emendation, as so many writers would (resenting everything the filmmaker does with his/her work save the check that it generates). Rather, Burgess embraced Kubrick's contribution to the emerging *Clockwork* super-genre and began referring to his most famous character as "Alex de Large" in post-1971 statements he made about the novel. At present, even readers of and professional critics interested in the novel routinely do likewise, even though the surname "de Large" doesn't occur in the novel.

As such, every time a contemporary novelist sits down and thinks, upon beginning to write, "Golly, I sure hope they make this into a movie" (a thought that would have been as inconceivable to Henry James, Marcel Proust, and Henry Fielding as it is common today); every time that same novelist sits down to write a novel and turns it into a screenplay instead (or vice versa as Cormac McCarthy did with *Cities of the Plain*); every time a screenwriter turns an unproduced script into a novel; and every time a director or producer scours the bestseller list in the West Coast-edition New York Times to find something out of which s/he can make a movie — every time such instances occur, novels, films, and their screenplay binding agent continue sloughing off whatever individual identities they might have once had, and instead, become something else entirely: a monstrous, three-headed genre that refuses, and in fact most likely cannot, resolve into a single whole. Such blatant incongruity, though, doesn't keep us from forcing the surprisingly functional match, nor does it keep our gruesome Ghidorah from efficaciously lumbering around the marketplace or the agora of ideas. Belching its hot spew into the future, leaving a wake of crumbled genre identities behind it, our monster does, however, represent a sort of prophetic fulfillment of the ancient and enduring suspicions we've always had about the instability of genre identity, especially as concerns sweet mother narrative. Keeping with this tradition, modern narrative's three-headed monster challenges what it means to create and consume narrative in the twenty-first century and, retrospectively, what it's always meant to separate one genre from another. And even as storytellers and story consumers move all around it, more or less unaware of the fire singeing our hair and the dominant place we've given our Ghidorah, we, like Yeats, have to face the fact that a terrible beauty has been born.

Quimby Melton lives in Southern California where he directs operations for his boutique hypermedia design firm Studio Hyperset (studiohyperset.com), co-edits SCRIPT (scriptjr.nl), and administers ia(¶) (inaparagraph.com). A graduate of the Universities of Georgia (BA, cum laude, '00) and Nevada, Las Vegas (MA, '03; PhD, '08), Quimby studied Anglo-American literature, 20th century art and music, and various new media technologies. He's published work in Bright Lights Film Journal, SCRIPT, and other publications. This essay was originally published in Bright Lights Film Journal 65 (August 2009, brightlightsfilm.com /65/65ghidorah.php [15 September 2010]).

Robert Levin

When Pacino's Hot, I'm Hot

Blanche Dubois always depended on the kindness of strangers. Me, I've always depended on strangers thinking I'm someone else.

I'm referring, in my case anyway, to getting sex.

I know it's weird, but the assumption some women make that I'm one or another of a certain group of actors and musicians has been, from my early adulthood to what's now my middle age, how I get my pipes cleaned more or less regularly and for free.

It's also made it possible for me to have (however briefly and if you're willing to stretch the definition) an actual relationship.

I should make it clear right away that on my own terms I'm not someone you'd describe as spilling over with attractive qualities. For one thing, a future with the second towel man in a car wash certainly isn't something a lot of women lie awake at night fantasizing about. No, it's not that I'm dumb; it's a problem that I have with applying and executing. I'm not good at those things. In fact, I'm terrible at them. I think this is because I've never been comfortable with the whole business of living. There's something unnatural about it that I find unsettling and I tend to lose my concentration in the least challenging of situations. You might want to indulge a generous impulse and remind me that anyone, on a given day, can screw up the Post Office test. But when I tell you that I also failed the New York City Transit Authority's dispatcher quiz, you'll have to agree that the condition of ineptitude here does for sure have a stunning dimension.

And if my level of achievement and corresponding financial circumstances aren't enough to give a lady pause, there's my appearance. Although I'm of Greek ancestry, the figure that I cut is something less than Greek. Just under average height, more skinny than slim, and with long, usually unkempt hair hanging over my ears and forehead and down the scruff of my neck, I also have heavily lidded eyes, sunken cheeks and a pallor that's cadaverous. While we may not be talking Elephant Man, this still isn't a picture I'd want to keep in *my* heart-shaped locket.

But here's the thing: When I look in the mirror I see (if a likeness is to be drawn at all) Ratso Rizzo or Sonny, the pathetic loser in *Scarecrow*. But a number of women, when they look at me, see Dustin Hoffman or Al Pacino. Or, for that matter, Bob Dylan and Leonard Cohen, among others.

Typically, and on an average of once a month, I'll be in a bar, seated alone in a corner and nursing a beer when, just like that, a woman will be at my shoulder.

"I know this is rude," she will say, "but I couldn't help myself. I had to come over to tell you how mesmerizing you were in *Godfather II*."

Or: "'Positively Fourth Street' — it changed my life!"

I realized some years later that the "strange thing" (as I came to call it) surfaced for the first time when I was only twelve. A dozen or so teenage girls were exiting a theater that was playing *A Hard Day's Night*. As I passed by on the other side of the street, one shouted something and then three or four of them broke from the others and began to run in my direction. I can recall my sensory equipment registering a small blip that this wasn't necessarily a bad thing. But terrified by their shrieks and the predatory way they were licking their lips, my reaction was to flee.

Nine years would pass before anything remotely comparable happened again, but by then, though no less mystified by what was taking place, I was at least ready to respond more appropriately.

Two weeks after my twenty-first birthday (and just one week after my graduation from high school), I was working as a messenger and in a cab on a summer morning with a package to deliver. Heading across town we were paused at a light when an incredible creature materialized. Wire thin, without a curve or a bump in her entire torso, and all arms and legs (especially legs — in my memory, doubtless distorted by time, her skirt is hemmed at just under her chin), she had to have been seven feet tall, and I'm not even counting the fuck-me heels and tendril-like spikes of hair that, drooping just a bit at the ends and gently waving as she moved, erupted from the top of her head. Factoring in the enormous sunglasses she was sporting on an oval face, she resembled nothing so much as a giant insect.

Coming alongside the cab, she did a broad double take, exclaimed, "Holy shit, I don't believe this," and yanked the door open. The light was still red when, tucking me back into my pants, she said, "Say 'hi' to Miss Baez for me, Bobby."

(I remember that my driver was holding both sides of his head with his hands and that his eyes were popping out like cartoon eyes on springs. When we arrived at my destination he not only refused to take any money, he actually gave *me* a roll of quarters.)

I still had no reason to regard this incident as anything more than a bizarre and isolated case of mistaken identity, until I encountered, a couple of weeks later in a bar, another woman who was under the impression I was Bob Dylan — and then another who was thoroughly persuaded that I was Al Pacino. With these events I could hardly fail to recognize the pattern that was developing.

Of course it would be awhile before I got a handle on the amazing gift I'd been handed and was able to realize something like its full potential. But in much the same way that I finally achieved respectable levels of competency in toilet procedures and at masturbating by myself, determination, practice and a willingness to learn from my mistakes paid off and I became increasingly proficient at utilizing it.

In the first of the instances I've just noted, for example, my response to the woman who approached me was to thank her for the implicit compliment and then to correct her. But when I observed that being truthful didn't just dampen her interest in me but provoked a discernible hostility — when, that is, she put her cigarette out in my drink and called me an "asshole" — I understood that denying the identity a woman assigned me was not the way to go and that I'd do well in the future to stifle the reflex to be honest.

And bearing this lesson in mind on the second occasion, I did get the girl to come back to my place.

Now before I go on I should point out that my place isn't exactly a showplace. It suits my budget, but it's in an old Lower East Side building where the facilities aren't in their conventional locations. (We're talking bathtub in the living room, toilet in the kitchen, that sort of thing.) Plus, I share the joint with several legions of cockroaches, an ever-extending family of rodents and an apparently unprecedented and aerodynamic hybrid of the two. (The biologists who've come from everywhere to investigate this phenomenon always leave with very concerned expressions on their faces.)

So as you've no doubt gathered, bringing a woman home was a really bad move. I'd go into detail about what took place when we arrived at my apartment, but since the matter is still in litigation it's probably wise to say only that (as I got it explained to me later) it was almost certainly the sudden presence of a total stranger, especially one with red hair, that precipitated the attack. (Apparently the creature was acting on some primal imperative to protect its young.) Okay? In my judgment it was more of a menacing and hovering thing than what you'd call an "attack." But I think that's all I'd better say about it.

Despite the unpleasantness, however, this episode was an important learning experience, and when yet another woman who believed I was Al Pacino presented herself I not only made no protest but insisted that we repair to *her* place. Well, a few hours later I was cheerfully extracting my shorts from a tangled mix of hastily discarded clothing at the foot of her bed (and promising that first thing in the morning I would instruct my agent to forward a signed eight-by-ten glossy from *Bobby Deerfield*).

But my education was hardly completed. If, at this point, I had two basic rules to follow — never volunteer the truth about myself and never let a woman anywhere near my apartment — I would soon recognize the need for a third: Never even think about *initiating* a hook-up. I'm referring here to events that took place on an evening when, horny enough to jerk off to a postcard of the Statue of Liberty but attracting no attention, I approached a woman and boldly introduced myself as Al Pacino. The loosened retina I sustained (and which makes everything get like very white for a second) has served to keep me mindful of just how critical to my success, not to mention my well being, is the discipline of laying back.

Yes (this is as good a point to deal with it as any), I did feel a little guilty at first. But I got over it.

Look, I know what you're thinking. You're thinking that what I do isn't nice, that I take advantage of the women I connect with.

Do you know what I want to say when I hear that? I want to say, *"FUCK YOU!"* — that's what I want to say. I've given the matter a great deal of thought and I'll explain this just once. The women I attract are not what you'd call off the top shelf. Though they all qualify as women in the technical sense, are all, that is, in possession of the crucial anatomical components (which, more often than not, are in something like a normal configuration), they are not exactly achingly beautiful, beaming with mental health or candidates for a Star Fleet Academy scholarship. In fact, and without exception, they are pretty desperate people, sick puppies and three-legged cat types. Many of them suffer horrendous hygiene problems and are also myopic to the point of posing a serious threat to themselves. They are usually very drunk as well. Given their condition the service I provide them is every bit as valuable as what they do for me.

Now don't understand me too fast — I'm not talking about providing them with sex. I'm talking about helping them satisfy another need, a need that's just as real and urgent as the need for sex. I'm talking, of course, about the need to feel special. By physically connecting to my celebrity these women can feel that they are sharing in my anointment.

But that's not all. After suffering the consequences of being truthful, and noticing over time that what questions they would ask me could, for the most part, be readily answered by any faithful viewer of "Entertainment Tonight," it gradually became clear to me that somewhere in their brains these women understood that I wasn't the luminary they were taking me for. But given how pressing was their need to rise above their abject circumstances, even for a minute (and something — whatever it was — about my physiognomy enabling them to use me to this purpose), the fact that they sort of knew they were delusional wasn't about to interfere with their pursuit of me.

So, as you can see, there's no exploiting going on here — not from my end anyway. I mean the very last thing these women wanted me to be was straight with them. On the contrary. They were counting on me to help them finesse a trick they were playing on themselves.

A trick they were playing on themselves! Get it?

Okay. I didn't mean to get vicious there, but since it's never really *me* who gets laid, I suffer kind of a large indignity myself. So I think people might find it within themselves to be, you know, a little less judgmental.

In any case, with the recognition that my role in the process was just to show up and play along, other methods of procedure I would over time develop are quite simple, intended only to make sure that I'm presenting myself in a way that's as amenable to distortion as I can get it and then to forestall the possibility of ruining things.

My manner of dress, for example. To try and stay apace of what some half-dozen affluent and more or less fashion-conscious men might be wearing at any given time would have been out of the question even if I'd been able to afford it. And since I never know who I'll be before I venture outside, whose wardrobe would I choose? So in the summer I wear jeans and a work shirt and either sneakers or boots. In the winter I add a sweater and a pea coat. I might very well be the complete non-entity and total loser that I am. On the other hand I could just as easily be a Master of the Universe in a casual mode.

My demeanor is informed by the same psychology. Once a woman has established contact I try to limit my responses to those rare questions I have no answer for to an ambiguous smile. Or, when I think it's best, I become silent and expressionless. Real actors will notice that, in the latter respect, I avail myself of a rudimentary device of their craft. Taking on a poker face, I let the woman read into it what her wishes and expectations dictate and require.

And, of course, no matter how agreeable the experience and melancholy the break, I always make it a point to disappear after one night.

With just one notable exception, I've scrupulously adhered to these rules and they've helped to assure me a fairly decent range of experiences.

I'm thinking now of a woman who despite an off-putting peccadillo that she had of blowing her nose with her hair, kept my interest by taking me through not just every position in the Kama Sutra but more than enough new ones to justify a supplementary volume. (It being Lou Reed's turn to get lucky I was serenaded all the while by her tape of my "Greatest Hits.")

I'm thinking as well of the time identical triplets, appropriately sharing the same delusion and built like middle linebackers, invited Leonard Cohen to a cluster fuck and wound up breaking two of my ribs.

It's a little off to the side, but I'm also thinking of a period that lasted several months during which I was continually approached by men. "I really enjoyed your work in *Cocks 'n' Cocks*, they would say. And they would go on to tell me how impressed they were by the way I took "full occupation" of my "space." That sort of thing.

It was puzzling. I'd never heard of this film, or of the actor — Johnson something — they were taking me for. At first uncomfortable with their advances, it dawned on me one evening that my chances for scoring had suddenly doubled and that I'd be a fool not to take advantage of this turn of events. (I mean where's the problem? It's just friction, isn't it?) But sad to say, not much would develop for me in this area. Before anything happened these guys would erupt in fits of incapacitating laughter, get really nasty or become crestfallen and disconsolate. It turned out that they'd decided I was Johnson Johnson, a porn actor who (within his discipline) was having his fifteen minutes. Curious, I found *Cocks 'n' Cocks* in a theater off Times Square and checked him out. To my surprise there were real and striking similarities between us — many more, in fact, than was usually so. Unfortunately there was also one significant difference. I had barely qualified for the "Woman's Home Companion" category in the old high school joke. When Johnson Johnson used the urinal in a men's room he probably had to stand in the hall.

And then there's the "relationship" I spoke of, which was also the time I broke most all of my rules. We're going back a dozen years here, but there are still nights during which I'm abruptly awakened by the sound of my voice calling her name. When I'm not alone these outbursts cause my bedmates to awaken rather abruptly themselves, but I think at least a part of what they find disconcerting is that the name I call is "Roger" — her father wanted a boy and he hadn't taken no for an answer.

A sparrow of a girl, no more than four-foot-ten and alarmingly skinny, Roger had thick black hair that, falling over most of her face, also fell nearly to the floor. The first time I saw her, from the other end of a long and crowded bar, I thought she was a half-opened umbrella standing on its handle.

We were introduced later that evening by a casual acquaintance of mine she turned out to be with and who was obviously trying to dump her. But when he said, and quite clearly I thought, "Roger, I'd like you to meet Pete Papadopolous," her reply was: "Mr. *Hoffman!* What an honorary and spectaculated phenomination. This is *peerless* even."

Now the thing was that when I saw what was happening normal procedure in this circumstance went out the window. I think I knew immediately that Roger was a keeper and at once recognizing how much she wanted me to be Hoffman and deathly afraid that she would turn away at the slightest hint that I wasn't (which would have been difficult to tell since her hair made it all but impossible to know in which direction she was facing), I went out of my way to nourish and perpetuate the "misunderstanding."

What can I say? I was in love for the only time in my life, and when, in our initial embrace a couple of hours later I must have squeezed her too hard and she urinated all over my sneakers, I just — I guess it was the intimacy of it — went over the top. Indeed, before the sun came up I had invited her to live with me and she had accepted.

"I'm so excrutiated," she gushed. "I'm besides both sides of myself. And yours too!"

Yes, of course I knew there was no way it could work, that it had to end badly. But I couldn't help entertaining the fantasy that if I drew her in really tight before she discovered her error, we might achieve a depth of bonding that would make my true identity (or lack of one) irrelevant.

The following morning (and amazed by the soothing effect her presence was having on my flying roommates — who'd stopped fluttering around so much and were making sweet cooing sounds), I was more than anxious to know everything about her.

She hadn't, I learned, had an easy time of it.

Her father, she said, had been a profligater of languigistics at a presticated universalment but had quit his tender position and dispassionated — just, and poignantly, a day after Roger, then a toddler, had spoken her first paragraph.

And truly heartbreaking, her mother, on whose insurance policy she'd been living for the last twenty years, had tragicastically electrified herself when she inexplaciously dropped a George Foreman grill into the bath she was taking — this on the evening of the day she'd come to Roger's first grade class to hear her recite "Mary Kept A Smallish Lamb."

But at that point (and apparently wrestling with her delusion — which was something I'd never known any of my women to do and which, I thought, said something about the quality of her character, though I'm not sure what exactly), she began to ask some questions of her own.

"How come you don't seem to have the majority of cash I respected?" she said. "How come you don't habituate in a nice place? How come you don't have a phone in case Steven Spielberg and Sidney Pollack are in a communicable way? How come your closet is only fulminating with jeans? Also, how come you don't keep your birds in cages?"

Considering that I wasn't used to such an interrogation — and that I was obliged to think on my feet — I came up with something that I thought wasn't bad.

"Honey," I said, "you've entered my life at the worst possible time and while I know that it's asking a lot, I can only hope you'll find it within yourself to bear with me. I'm afraid that I may be afflicted with what's called the 'J.D. Salinger Syndrome'. It's a condition of creative paralysis that sometimes develops in artists who have achieved a legendary stature. Owning the prospect of a fame that will survive their demise, they live in terror of losing that prospect by producing work that might be inferior to what they've already accomplished. Rather than risk tainting their image, they cease to function and, in the worst cases, to even appear in public where the possibility of a clumsy or mediocre utterance could alter and diminish the way they're perceived. What happens is that they effectively sacrifice the remainder of their lives to their immortality. I may or may not overcome this disease and I'll understand completely if its something you want no part of. All I can say is that I'm deliberately staying out of the public eye right now and that I've cut myself off from even my closest friends and associates who, meaning well but not understanding, would only make light of my problem and encourage me to work. This unfortunately includes my accountant who happens to be the only person with access to my bank accounts. As for the apartment, it's my hideout. It's perfect as a hideout because no one would ever think to look for me in such a crummy place. You're the only one who knows about it, the only person I've trusted enough to bring to it. But again, I'll understand if this isn't something you want to involve yourself with because it won't be a whole lot of fun and I don't know how it will end."

And it worked. Roger said nothing, but in addition to breaking out in a really hideous rash as I spoke, her chest swelled noticeably, almost expanding into something like a bosom. She must have felt five feet tall to be deemed worthy of sharing in my time of trial.

But her obvious uneasiness with the situation in which she found herself would periodically surface. A couple of days later she wanted to know why more people didn't notarize me on the street.

"Really good actors," I said, "have the ability to be anonymous when they want to be, sometimes even invisible."

I remember that when I said this it made her giggle.

But even putting aside the considerable tensions caused by my charade (and the always stressful necessity to invent places I was going to when I left the house for the car wash every day), living with Roger was nerve-racking all by itself — like being tuned to two radio stations at once in a room with the light bulb loose in its socket. Periods of incessant chatter, for instance, would suddenly be interrupted, often in mid-sentence, by a dead silence, as though her plug had been pulled from the wall. At such times she might become motionless as well. Although her eyes would remain open I couldn't be sure if she was actually conscious. In fact, on several occasions, I'd have been ready to believe she'd expired were it not for an odd clucking sound, the origin of which I was never able to locate, and something unattractive that she did with the muscles around her mouth.

Still, as enormous as the problems were, the moments of bliss I experienced in those first weeks more than compensated for them.

Spring was beginning and, celebrating its arrival, we did the things new lovers do when spring is upon them. We went to a windswept beach where we romped and frolicked in the sand. Locked in an embrace we rolled over and over down a steep hill in Central Park. In the evenings I washed her hair and she gleefully folded my penis into woodland animal shapes.

I'd have to say that, all things considered, life was pretty good.

Then it went bad.

Roger read in a newspaper that Hoffman was going to shoot a film somewhere in the Midwest and that he'd be on location for two weeks.

"Why didn't you jerk my head up?" she said, showing me the article.

Even though I'd known all along that such a development was inevitable, I was nonetheless shaken by this news. It took no small effort to collect myself sufficiently to say: "I was going to tell you, but I thought I'd wait until the last minute because I wasn't sure the part would work out and because I knew how painful a separation now will be for us. I didn't want to make you sad before I had to."

But she was happy. Clapping her hands she said, "I'm so glad to know you lastly clambered over your jaded salanjastiker hippodrome."

"Well let's not get ahead of ourselves," I said. "It could be just a fleeting thing."

Needing a place to get lost for two weeks, and with nowhere else to go, it was left for me to seek accommodations at the car wash. And the night before I departed Roger helped me pack my things. When we were done she went to the kitchen and brought back a bottle of cheap champagne she'd concealed in the back of the refrigerator.

"This is a time for jubilating," she said, pulling the cork herself. Then, touching my glass with hers, she said, "Breakfast with eggs, Duster!"

As you can imagine, the following days were either bad or worse than bad. Sleeping in various vehicles in a lot adjoining the wash, I showered and did my laundry standing behind cars on the conveyor belt. And missing her terribly, the fact that I couldn't call the apartment because I'd never been able to afford a phone was torture for me. I could only hope that she was okay.

Finally, mercifully, the two weeks were up and I went home.

Hearing my key in the lock, Roger came to the door holding a newspaper and with one of my "birds" perched on top of her head. Without a word, she shoved the paper at me before I'd even crossed the threshold. It was open to a story about Hoffman. Some kind of budget issue had arisen and production on his film had been suspended. During the hiatus Hoffman was staying in New York. The paper had been printed on the date he arrived.

He'd been here for a *week!*

Putting the paper down I met her eyes and saw that they were red and swollen.

"Where were you?" she said. "A whole plus seven — and twenty-four as well."

When I had no quick answer she said, "You're doing an exquisite triathlon, isn't it?"

You will appreciate that, as heart wrenching as her question was, my principle emotion at that moment was relief.

"Darling, Darling," I said, "No way. There's no way I would ever betray you like that. No, I'm not having an illicit liaison. How could you think such a thing? I'm playing an unhappy man and to stay in character I deprived myself of your company — for as long as I could bear it anyway. It's just a coincidence that it was exactly one week.

Roger stepped toward me and buried her face in my abdomen.

"I was frightful," she said

She was trembling and so was I. We stood holding each other for a very long time.

Determined from then on to be more careful, I made a special effort to monitor what she might read, see or hear. But I couldn't cover everything. Just a few days later we were awakened by the radio alarm clock and immediately heard on a newscast that the budget problem had been resolved and that Hoffman was back on location. Fleeing to the kitchen to find something to kill myself with, I could feel Roger right behind me. I expected flying dishes. What I got was a juicy kiss.

"You didn't have to submit a misleader about being Dustin Hoffman," she said. "Why did you think you had to be duplicacious with me?"

I was stunned. Had my wildest dreams come true? Was it possible that Roger had come to love me for myself after all? I couldn't believe it. Nor could I believe the sex that was to follow.

I always knew Roger was hot when (it was her signal to me) she lay down on the bed on her stomach, raised her skirt and floated an air biscuit. But that morning's air biscuit resonates for me to this day. Indeed, it will be forever etched in my memory, not only for its remarkable housekeeping application (it worked to clear the apartment of all vermin for almost a month), but because it served to set the stage for the most incredible orgasm I've ever had.

I've never been able to faithfully describe that orgasm. If I report that before it I'd had no idea how much sheer joy there was to feel in sex, that never in my life have I known so pure an ecstasy, I don't begin to do it justice or to convey how, in the throes of it, I felt myself transported to a place beyond time and that, floating free as something like total spirit, I was privy for an instant to the deepest secrets and most puzzling mysteries of creation. (In that apocalyptic moment I actually understood, for example, why Chuck Norris was on the planet.)

And I can say this notwithstanding the fact that the orgasm was somewhat premature — I was still standing over the bed and fully clothed when it happened.

Anyway, when it was done and I lay down next to her, happily exhausted, basking in the afterglow, I was ready to drop my guard and reveal my true self to her in all its emptiness. Brushing away her hair to find her face, which took awhile, I was about to speak when she said:

"You'll never assume the crush I had for you."

"?"

"I saw *Our Picnics in Needles Park* six times and *Bobby Dearest* eleven times. God, Alfredo, how I wanted to sit on your head!"

If, only minutes earlier, I'd discovered what it must feel like to win the lottery, now I knew the depths of despair. Even to think about commencing a new deception was beyond my strength.

I didn't know what to do.

Just a few days later, and too weary at this point to bother checking the TV listings, the matter was taken from my hands. Pacino suddenly turned up on a live talk show we were watching. When he came on, Roger looked at me, then back at the screen and then at me again.

"How are you doing that?" she said.

When I could only shrug she bolted from the room and was gone for twenty minutes. She must have lapsed into her semiconscious thing because I could hear that strange clucking sound (which was a lot louder than usual). When she returned she stood directly in front of me with her arms akimbo. (I could tell her arms were akimbo because her elbows were sticking out of her hair at the same 45-degree angle.)

This time there was no mistaking it, she was pissed.

"You haven't been Al Pacino either," she said.

"No, Honey, I haven't."

Where once Roger had contemplated me with an unabashed reverence, as though an aureole surrounded my face, now she looked at me as though I was the lowest form of nature's creepy crawly creations.

"You're a pathoprecocious person," she said. You're a hypothetical liar. Well, don't bother to make up something improved because it'll be too little and without much else."

"Sweetheart . . . "

"I mean it," she said. "I'm cognisacious of the person you really are now. I've been expecting it for days."

Yes, I was ready to say ruefully, I'm Fred the Fraud. I'm Sid the Shit. I'm Deforest the Deceiver.

"You're *Emilio Estevez*," she said. "You're Emilio Estevez and you're ashamed of yourself. Why? Why, Emilio? I know you aren't a word that people keep inside the house, but yesterday when my suspicionings aroused me and I said to myself, 'Roger, you're a chimp, this can't be broccoli you're smelling', I went to a laberarium and found you in a book. It said you were a 'thirdly ratinated thespassian who sometimes didn't stink up the place'. Wouldn't I co-habituate with Emilio

Estevez? Am I so stuffed-up, or what the fuck is this?"

"Rog . . . "

"If only you'd had the retegritude to level yourself for me. But now . . . . Oh Emilio, I could never stay with a man who has so weenie an irregardlessness for his oral fibers. Nor I myself."

I pleaded with her not to go. I had no way to pull it off, of course, but I promised to take her backstage to meet the cast of *Cats*. I know she agonized over the proposal, but this lady was not without principles. Indeed, she looked at me then as though it was a few years after Watergate and I was Richard Nixon wondering aloud to Republican Party officials if they might, you know, consider nominating me again.

A few months later Roger took up with a guy she's been with ever since. I think she thinks he's Danny DeVito and I've often wondered, since they have a phone, how he handles it when Jack Nicholson and Michael Douglas never call.

And while I'm on a sour note anyway I might as well tell you of a period in which the celebrity connection women make for me actually worked to my detriment. It was when Pacino's *Revolution* was released — and on its heels the video. Amounting to a devastating left jab, right cross combination, these unfortunate events threatened to end my career as well as Pacino's. In fact, it got so bad for a while that even women who thought I was Gabriel Byrne would suddenly back off and decide to take a pass. It really wasn't until *Sea of Love* revived Pacino's popularity that I got hot again.

When I look back, however, it's clear to me that even during that difficult interval I was better off than I would otherwise have been and I know that I have nothing to complain about. Although I may not have compiled Hall of Fame-level stats, neither has my life been bereft of carnal experiences.

Moreover, I got a woman to actually live with me and though it was very brief, that union produced a son. (Unbeknownst to us at the time, Roger was pregnant when she left me.) I haven't mentioned my son because frankly he embarrasses even me. To say it as gently as I can, most people, when they've seen him or tried to engage him in conversation, take for granted that his parents were first cousins. But Eileen (Roger wanted a girl and she wouldn't take no for an answer) is almost a teenager now and I've noticed lately, when he comes to visit and we're out on the street, that he's begun to turn the head of more than an occasional young lady.

Here's wishing whoever they want him to be a very long run.

Robert Levin is the coauthor and coeditor, respectively, of two collections of essays about jazz and rock in the '60s: Music & Politics (with John Sinclair), World, and Giants of Black Music (with Pauline Rivelli), Da Capo Press. Among numerous other places, his stories and commentary have appeared in, or on the web sites of, Absinthe Literary Review, Best of Nuvein Fiction, Cosmoetica, Eyeshot, New York Review, Rolling Stone, Sein und Werden, Sweet Fancy Moses, Underground Voices, Unlikely Stories, The Village Voice and the Word Riot 2003 Anthology.

Carlos Amantea

Cousin Hans

The last time I played doctor with anyone — I mean really played doctor — it was with my sister Leslie. She was sort of a pill about it, if you want to know the truth: bossing me around, put your legs up, lean over, turn around — just like a real doctor. I didn't enjoy it too much.

The time before that was with Cousin Hans. That was more fun, for sure. Hans was too mild to be bossing anyone around. He just wanted to show off some new and awesome parts of his physique, and, I have to admit, it did take my breath away. He was thirteen and I was twelve, and his bag-of-tricks had blossomed in a most fascinating way, with a few plums down there and a banana or so over here, everything overlaid with the most gorgeous blue-black bouquet garni. It was a treat.

To our mutual regret, we didn't get to fiddle around because shortly after the pants dropped, someone slammed a door downstairs and we were both of us dressed and out in the hall and outside in a trice. Turned out it was only the wind.

Cousin Hans and I had a chance to meet later under less auspicious circumstances. It was at an Easter party for the family. He and I talked of this and that, and I was toying with the idea of bringing up a few memories, but there was much family milling about. Part of the problem was that in the interim (three decades) Hans had been called to the service of the cloth, and was now doctoring to the spiritual needs of a small Episcopalian congregation just outside Bushnell, Florida.

Hans had overcome his past shyness, both in talk and gesture — and, in the process, had taken on a bride. She was already heavy with child. Upon meeting me, she gave me the requisite cousin-in-law kiss, and told me, small black burning eyes fixed just above my brow, that Hans had told her a lot about me. "Not too much, I hope," I said, with a pleasantly faked laugh.

It was one of those festive family gatherings, filled with too much food, drink, and strained camaraderie. Hans — or I should say Reverend Hans — was wearing a high white collar that seemed about to choke him, making his face unseasonably red, and his eyes started out of his head like a ferret, what little I could see of them (he affected some brown-gray tinted, rimless glasses). In addition, the black uniform (clerical shirt, black leather belt, black pants, black shoes, black socks) tended to emphasize his considerable girth, so I felt myself to be conversing with a double-decker Easter egg, red-on-black. All this did not lend itself to an easy exchange of confidence, especially some misty past intimacy.

Rev. Hans told me that he had a sermon on Communism which was quite popular with his congregation. He asked if he could send me a tape of his sermon, and I said I would be delighted.

He went on ahead, during dinner, to give me a blow-by-blow precis of the sermon. Between eight (eight!) chicken thighs, fried in lard, and four helpings of mashed potatoes (butter gravy) and three servings of black-eyed peas, he described in some detail the Communist Menace. Dessert found us with Reds all over the Brown Betty I mean the library system, knee-deep in Marxist hard sauce I mean teachers. He turned down the sweet liqueur, perhaps because he didn't want to seem unwatchful, for even a moment. He said it was bad for his heart.

* * * *

Cousin Hans' spectacles did something funny to my heart, I can tell you. The last time I had seen brown-tinted glasses, the bottoms rounded like tear-drops, was on the face of Cousin Hans' father, the man we called, appropriately enough, Big Hans.

Big Hans and Aunt Irma and Cousin Hans live ten blocks up from our house, on Talbot Avenue, just off Kraft Circle. It is 1939, just before we are to embark on the last of our great series of World Wars. The house is a three-bedroom stucco variety, very white and pretty outside, very dark and moveless inside. All the curtains are drawn, and the blinds are down, and all the doors are shut. This is to keep out the summer heat and any small boys with mud on their shoes. Cousin Hans is an only child: he is seven and I — his constant and faithful companion — am six.

Aunt Irma, the one who keeps all the doors shut, uses a great deal of face powder, so that her coal-dark eyes seem to be peering at us from behind a child's mask of pink-and-white. Her front teeth are angled at a partial ell, giving her the mouth of a chipmunk. When she laughs, she rolls her eyes upwards as if to check with the Divine for her levity.

Cousin Hans is called "Buddy" to distinguish him from the man thirty years and two-hundred-and-fifty pounds his senior. Big Hans' eyes, as I have said, never seem to change as he peers at me, at Buddy, at the world, with that tint of steel. His hands are large but his fingers are strangely tiny, making them look like the doctor's rubber gloves when we blew them up to make balloons.

There is a picture of Buddy in the living room. It is a photograph taken shortly after some religious rite which formally inducted him into Episcopalian Church. In his white jacket and shorts, with the halo bleached-out effect surrounding his whole body, he seems to be floating in a cloud of divinity. Since we were so seldom permitted in "the front room," his picture takes on added stature as some religious icon, the picture of The Perfect Buddy, the Holy Child, my friend at a rare time of perfection.

Given his angelic appearance, you would think that Buddy couldn't be a problem to anyone. Evidently, however, something is amiss. This is attested to by the sheer number of times that Big Hans works over Buddy with his leather belt. When he is beaten, Cousin Hans howls out "wowwow-wow." Even now, so many years later, I can hear the swish of belt through air, the whack on Buddy's bare behind (Uncle Hans made him drop his pants and underpants — and bend over and grab his ankles) and Buddy howling "wow-wow*WOW-WOW*."

I had then, I have now, a record of *Alice in Wonderland,* the 1935 movie out of Hollywood. The record doubles as a round photograph of the production and I can see the duchess, wearing what appears to be a chasuble. She scowls out at me, peering from under an elaborate headdress, with double points — as if it were hiding two horns. When she spins around in a blur on the wind-up Victrola, I hear the song:

Speak roughly to your little boy,
And beat him when he sneezes,
He only does it to annoy,
Because he knows it teases . . . .

then the artiste, in a dignified voice, with a slight English accent, intones: Wow — wow — *wow wowwow!*

* * * *

It was a time, that time when I was growing up in the South, when the land was so washed in the light of the summer sun that it seems, as I look back on it now, that all shadows had been banished. The sun would come each day to blast the landscape, and at noon, the very birds would fall quiet in the manzanita oaks, as if the effort of singing were just too much.

Whenever I listen to that record, my mind's eye fills up with that image of me a child in the land of the blasted sun, and I hear the words of Lewis Carroll and I catch myself thinking of my friend Cousin Hans, aged seven, my friend Buddy who once stood so straight, my good kind funny rambunctious friend, the child-friend of mine, who would never hurt anyone, who never harmed leaf nor flower nor bug, who certainly would never ever harm me. I think on him, and I wondered then, as I do now, on him getting beaten, getting beaten so very much, with that heavy, black, shiny black belt that hangs on the hook on the inside of the door to the closet in his father's bedroom. My child's logic tries to explain the regular, never-ending beatings with, say, the sneezes, because, maybe, Big Hans does not want him to sneeze, because it annoys. But then my child's mind tells me that Cousin Hans doesn't sneeze any more than I do, and I don't get beaten, not at all. It must have something to do with *Alice in Wonderland* because I have another vision of Buddy, back in his father's bedroom, holding onto his ankles, already beginning to shake at the anticipated whipping (which seems to take forever to commence) and I have this picture in my mind of Big Hans pulling from the back of his closet this black wimple, with the two projections on the top, and a mask, with the face of the duchess painted on it, with the great dewlaps and the big jutting chin and the furrows across the brow. I see Big Hans dressing up in that costume before he goes to work with such painful force on Buddy's backside.

After the whippings (they always call it a "whipping" as in *Buddy, you're gonna get a whipping)* they come out, Buddy with red eyes, Uncle Hans with red face, and we would sit down for lunch of peanut butter and guava jelly sandwiches and big glasses of cold milk, and Big Hans tries to grab my hand under the table with his big meaty hands. He pretends to be a snake, and hisses through his teeth, and snatches at my legs under the table, and nods and winks at me behind those darkened specs. Buddy laughs through his tears, laughing at the way his father plays with me under the table.

* * * *

One day Buddy and I decide to burn the house down. We get underneath it, under the kitchen, in the crawl space, with the dirt below and the unfinished floor above. There is the acrid sharp smell of rat droppings, and the spiders spin out their days in corners of the joists. We bring in our matches and pine kindling and newspaper, and we set a regular First Class Boy Scout's bonfire. Carrie, the maid, who comes Tuesdays and Fridays to do the laundry, figures out something is wrong. She's slapping around the kitchen in her old shoes, the ones with the leather split at the sides to let the brown beetles, her toes, out at the sides, and as she comes to stand before the ironing board, she can feel the floor getting warmer and warmer under her feet.

She knows the furnace isn't on, it being 100-degree Florida summer outside, and as our flower of fire grows more and more grand, spewing out a great gray smoke, we start to cough and we can see, through our tears, Carrie's black legs striding back-and-forth in the yard, with the hem of her skirt jumping about, and then her face, upside-down, mooney eyes peering, straining to see into the cloudy darkness, and she's saying, "Buddy! What you doin' in there? Buddy! *BUDDY!*"

Buddy begs her not to tell, I beg her not to tell, we beg and beg. After all, our lives are at stake. We beg with great fervor, but she won't listen. Carrie is usually on our side, and will hide small misdeeds, but she evidently figures that this one is out of her domain, and she says, "Ah'm gonna have to tell Miz Milam . . ." and she does. When Aunt Irma comes home, we are sent out of the kitchen, and we sit on the back stairs. We have that caving feeling, that feeling in the stomach, of a dark and horrible thing awaiting us at the edge of the day, and nothing will make it go away. It is as inevitable to us as the move of the sun, and the rising tide of cicada songs that begin each evening, at five or so, and carries on into the evening. We huddle apart on the back steps, not wanting to think, or talk, and certainly not to play, what with this angry spiralling wrath of the gods awaiting us, this terrible thing which will rise about our heads, as surely as the sparks fly upwards, to consume us in its wrath.

We promise Aunt Irma especial fealty if she won't tell Big Hans. We dangle in front of her promises of eternal goodness, a goodness that, like a great heavenly stairway, will rise eternally into the future. Such angels we will be, sitting so quietly every day, she won't even know the two of us, we wrapped in white goodness, thanking everyone for every favor, being so polite and thoughtful.

We don't have a chance. She calls up Uncle Hans at the office, and there seems to be a long silence after she tells him about the fire, and the smoke, under the house, under the house she says over again, and in the silence I look at Buddy and he is looking as pale and drawn and hopeless as I have ever seen him. Since Uncle Hans works in the same office as my father, we know that we are doubly damned, it's going to be all over town, everyone and his brother will know about our Nero act. I tell Buddy that I really didn't want to do it, that it was his fault, that I told him we shouldn't do it, but he doesn't seem to hear me, doesn't even seem to know that I exist, his face so drawn, his hand up over his mouth holding his head up. With his hand he rocks his head back and forth, and his eyes are lost, distant, gone . . . .

* * * *

Buddy and I meet somewhat shamefacedly the next weekend, and when we are alone in his room, he drops his pants and shorts and shows me his backside. It's not just his buttocks, but, as well, the backs of his legs all the way down to knee-level, and up his back, half-way up to his shoulders. The whole area is a brilliant blue-black color with intermixed reds and purples. "Wow," I say. I had never seen such a coloring of the human body before. When Buddy sits — he seems to prefer standing much of the time — he would tend to favor one cheek or the other. His eyes are what have changed the most, though. They are, what? . . . more distant, more watery, less clearly focused. He seems preoccupied, as if he has something new or important to think about, and as we play, he seems listless, disinterested. There is none of the old gusto of run and catch and play and laugh. Rather, there is a strange distance from his self and being.

After that, Buddy seems to get punished more often. Uncle Hans and Aunt Irma are good church-going folk, going to the Ebing Court Episcopal Church. Buddy goes with them, of course, but they seem to feel that he has gotten a touch of the devil that they must physically evict from his body. He comes to be beaten for a strange variety of reasons. There is the time that someone drops a milk bottle on the sidewalk, in front of the house, where it shatters. Big Hans asks Buddy if he had done it, and I can remember Buddy, his voice rising in hysteria, saying he didn't, saying he didn't, saying please believe me, I didn't, please believe, I didn't . . . . But it is too late, and I remember sitting alone on the steps, hearing my seven-year-old friend crying out, begging his father to stop, please to stop, please, it hurts so.

I remember thinking that Buddy is caught in some maze spaghetti trap. He can do nothing, nothing at all, without violating some complex rule which none of us can quite figure out. We never know when we go down the stairs and play in the mud at the back of the house or pull each other about in the REO SpeedWagon — we are never sure that this simple act of playing might be violating some arcane rule in Big Hans' system which will bring down another painful series of retributions, the weight of which is so tremendous that Buddy has to cry out with all the force in his seven-year-old body, trying to get his father to believe that he has done nothing wrong, nothing wrong at all; and in this act of trying to convince him that he is not wrong, he is wrong, and must get punished for that. One day, I am out on Talbot Avenue, Buddy is somewhere behind me, and I lift up the cover to a water meter, to see what's down there in the darkness, and a hundred or so fire ants come bubbling forth, and I think that I had better put the cover back down, at once, because I think that if Uncle Hans finds out, he will beat Buddy yet again, for something that I did.

The last punishment I can remember is the one for Buddy's "attitude." It seems that Aunt Irma complained to Big Hans that Cousin Hans is talking to her with a tone of voice that doesn't seem respectful enough. As he is led into the backroom, Buddy is deathly silent. It is as if the charge is so monstrous that there is no defense, no defense at all for the way he talks, or speaks . . . for the way he *talks,* for the way he *speaks.*

After it is over, and we are eating our sandwiches and Famous Chocolate Wafer Cookies, Uncle Hans reaches for my leg under the table, and I try to get away from it, but I can't: there is no escaping from that big meaty hand with the tiny fingers, getting at me like some animal, with its large animal force.

* * * *

Within a month after I got back from the crowded and food-filled Easter Vacation at home, I got a small, three-inch reel of tape from The Bushnell Episcopalian Church. I auditioned it to check on the quality, and what I heard was a great deal of communal coughing and scratching and shuffling, with a low voice droning on in the distance somewhere. I could hear an occasional snatch of a word or two, and a thunderstorm of sound as the congregation rose to sing "Onward Christian Soldiers." I surmised that Reverend Hans had placed the microphone back at the back somewhere, say in the Baptismal Font.

I didn't have the heart to tell him, and I filed the tape in the desk drawer marked "Yesterday's Mashed Potatoes," and for all I know, it is still there, to this day, resting quietly and darkly along with the other secrets of our life which might well be better to leave in the quiet darkness, out of reach of the light and sun of memory which — after all — might only stain and fade them and make them totally unrecognizable.

Carlos Amantea wrote travel pieces for salon.com for several years, and currently writes for *The Review of Arts, Literature, Philosophy and the Humanities,* at www.ralphmag.org. His book on family therapy, *The Lourdes of Psychotherapy,* has been published by the Milton H. Erickson Foundation (and, as *El Lourdes de Arizona*, by Cuatros Vientos of Chile). It was nominated for the Pulitzer Prize in 1992.

Jesse Glass

Essay X

I'm really interested in shit. I mean, I know what you think. It isn't that way at all, but I like to look at it. Like my own. When you, you know, stand up and there it is. An apport from another dimension. Fascinating stuff. Sometimes you know you look at it and you say did I actually, you know, produce that thing? A minor miracle, if I could be so bold. Then, after a few mental notes — more archaeological than anything — a reluctant flush. When I'm walking along the sidewalk in any city (let's say, City X) and I see . . . there it is. A promise of something, like the rainbow after a storm. Like, I'm walking along on a bright fucking day. A really nice fucking day. Say, a sunny fucking day, with blue fucking skies and fucking cumulus clouds, plenty of them, and I'm whistling and thinking things aren't too goddamnned fucking bad. No, say I'm not whistling, that would be too much. Too much. I'm walking along, I pass one or two people. An old lady and a young lady, no doubt residents of City X. They're walking right along. Looking up. Looking away. They walk past me, and I notice the young lady suddenly . . . well she suddenly looks down and does a dance step. A step away and to the side. A one and a two. Like that. And she makes a slight face. I look past her small sign of disgust and there it is. Red. Brick red and lying in the middle of the sidewalk. Like a fallen menhir; as monumental as Stonehenge — no, that's too hyperbolic, isn't it — no, looking like something — an artifact — shaped by a proto-human — Pithecanthropus erectus, ok? And it's there and cracking in the heat. I mean, the second law of thermodynamics is obviously having its way. But it doesn't smell. It's been there too long to smell. Even the ants have stopped picking it apart. Flies no longer congregate. What or who did it? More than likely a large dog, but maybe not. Could have been human — a bum, maybe — who knows? — one of those business or lawyer types you see in gray suits with grayer faces — or, wait a minute — it could have been the pretty young lady. She squatted there and did it. Fall from innocence, and was returning to the scene of the crime, so to speak, to subtly point out the place of her fall. What could have compelled her to shit right there on the sidewalk, in the early hours of the morning, days, months — maybe eons ago? Rage? Fear? Frustration? And she was pretty. All that blonde hair. Perfumed too. Beautiful shortened upper lip, upturned nose. I couldn't believe it. Yet I got an insight into her — how shall I say it — soul? — because of her reaction of fear, of guilt. Yes, I had guessed her secret. It was almost as if I had possessed her, was possessing her at that very moment. She looked at me, flashed a — get this — flashed a smile. A nervous smile, mind you, and walked away, clitter clatter, on her high heels. Which were black. A smile pretty as you please. With the old lady nattering on about Schopenhauer. I mean, Schopenhauer? And she left me there with it, studying it, inferring her most intimate secrets from it. The evidence of the animality under her skirt. The beautiful long-legged beast. I thought I was the only one who continued to wage war against the body. I mean, the allurements of the body. Wear these plain old clothes. Steel-toed work shoes. But I give in as she did. Does. I wasn't alone in my need to reenact this terrible unlacing, uncrossing of the legs, loosing of the squalid valves of meat. Yes, yes. It was too much to be believed. I could have passed out right there. I could have eaten it.

Jesse Glass runs Ahadada Press. He's the author of Lost Poet: Four Plays (BlazeVox) and *The Passion of Phineas Gage & selected poems* (West House Books).

ND - #0500 - 270225 - C0 - 229/152/15 - PB - 9781907133152 - Matt Lamination